Teaching Resources F

Unit Seven: Literature in Modern America
(Modern Nonfiction and Modern Drama)

to accompany

Adventures
in American Literature

ATHENA EDITION

HOLT, RINEHART AND WINSTON
Harcourt Brace & Company

Austin · New York · Orlando · Chicago · Atlanta · San Francisco · Boston · Dallas · Toronto · London

Printed in the United States of America

ISBN 0-03-095466-5

1 2 3 4 5 6 7 8 9   082   99 98 97 96 95 94

TABLE OF CONTENTS

UNIT SEVEN: LITERATURE IN MODERN AMERICA

MODERN NONFICTION

Teacher's Notes 1
Study Guide 2
Selection Test 4

WALDEN (JUNE 1939) *E. B. White*

Teacher's Notes 6
Reading Check 9
Study Guide 10
Building Vocabulary 13

THE CREATIVE PROCESS *James Baldwin*

Teacher's Notes 14
Reading Check 16
Study Guide 17
Language Skills 19
Building Vocabulary 22
Selection Test (E.B. White *and* James Baldwin) 24

NOBEL PRIZE ACCEPTANCE SPEECH *William Faulkner*

Teacher's Notes 25
Reading Check 27
Study Guide 28
Building Vocabulary 30
Selection Test (James Baldwin *and* William Faulkner) 32

THIS WRITER'S SENSE OF PLACE
Rolando R. Hinojosa-Smith

Teacher's Notes 33
Study Guide 36
Language Skills 39
Building Vocabulary 41
Selection Vocabulary Test 43
Selection Test (William Faulkner *and* Rolando R. Hinojosa-Smith) 44

NOBEL LECTURE IN LITERATURE   *Toni Morrison*

Teacher's Notes 45
Study Guide 46
Building Vocabulary. 48

TIN LIZZIE   *John Dos Passos*

Teacher's Notes 49
Reading Check. 51
Study Guide 52

from DUST TRACKS ON A ROAD   *Zora Neale Hurston*

Teacher's Notes 54
Study Guide 56
Language Skills 59
Building Vocabulary. 62

CIRCUS AT DAWN   *Thomas Wolfe*

Teacher's Notes 64
Reading Check. 66
Study Guide 67

from BLACK BOY   *Richard Wright*

Teacher's Notes 69
Reading Check. 71
Study Guide 72
Building Vocabulary. 74

from THE WAY TO RAINY MOUNTAIN
N. Scott Momaday

Teacher's Notes 76
Reading Check. 79
Study Guide 80
Building Vocabulary A. 82
Building Vocabulary B. 85
Selection Test   (John Dos Passos, Zora Neale Hurston, Thomas Wolfe,
   Richard Wright, *and* N. Scott Momaday) 86

MOTHER TONGUE   *Amy Tan*

Teacher's Notes 87
Reading Check. 89
Study Guide 90
Language Skills 92

THE NAMES OF WOMEN *Louise Erdrich*

    Teacher's Notes 95
    Reading Check. 97
    Study Guide 98
    Selection Test 100

UNIT ASSESSMENT STRATEGIES

    Teacher's Notes 102
    Mastery Test 104
    Analogy Test. 106
    Composition Test. 108

UNIT SEVEN: LITERATURE IN MODERN AMERICA

MODERN DRAMA

    Teacher's Notes 110
    Study Guide 112
    Selection Test 114

TRIFLES *Susan Glaspell*

    Teacher's Notes 116
    Study Guide 119
    Language Skills 121
    Building Vocabulary. 124
    Selection Test 126

WHERE THE CROSS IS MADE *Eugene O'Neill*

    Teacher's Notes 128
    Study Guide 131
    Language Skills 133
    Building Vocabulary. 136
    Selection Test 138

OUR TOWN *Thornton Wilder*

    Teacher's Notes 140
    Reading Check (Act One) 145
    Reading Check (Act Two) 146
    Reading Check (Act Three) 147
    Study Guide 148
    Language Skills 152
    Building Vocabulary. 155
    Selection Test 157

UNIT ASSESSMENT STRATEGIES

Teacher's Notes 159
Mastery Test 161
Analogy Test 165
Composition Test 167

TO THE TEACHER

This booklet, *Teaching Resources F,* contains unit and selection teaching suggestions as well as a wide variety of materials that can be used to enliven instruction, address specific curriculum concerns, attend to individual student needs, and monitor student mastery.

SELECTION TEACHING MATERIALS

Teaching Notes with Answer Keys—Teaching suggestions and useful instructional features are found on the **Teacher's Notes** pages that are provided for almost every individual literary selection. The **Teacher's Notes** for a specific selection may contain a variety of the following features:

- itemized **Objectives** for teaching the selection
- an **Introduction** to the selection, with helpful background details about the author, the literary period, or the literary work
- critical or scholarly **Commentary** about the selection
- a **Reading/Critical Thinking Strategies** feature to lead students into, through, and beyond the meaning of the literary selection
- a list of **Vocabulary** words from the selection that are defined in the glossary in the textbook, along with the textbook page number or the poem line number on which each word is to be found
- a **Vocabulary Activity** to support study of the selection and development of the student's vocabulary skills

In addition to these features, the **Teacher's Notes** pages contain **Answer Keys** to worksheets that are provided to support study of a particular selection.

Copying Masters/Student Worksheets—These worksheets and support materials may include a variety of the following types of copying masters:

- **Reading Check** worksheets—provide comprehensive questions that help confirm student understanding of the meaning of the selection
- **Study Guide** worksheets—contain a series of leading questions that guide students through a close analytical reading of the selection
- **Language Skills** worksheets—contain exercises that often use brief excerpts from the literary selection to integrate grade-level-appropriate language, grammar, usage, and mechanics skills
- **Building Vocabulary** worksheets—offer a range of strategies to help students acquire vocabulary-improvement skills
- **Selection Vocabulary Tests**—provide a check of student mastery of the vocabulary words found in the selection
- **Selection Tests**—help to evaluate student understanding of the literary selection

UNIT TEACHING MATERIALS

Support materials for assessing unit mastery may include the following copying masters:

- **Mastery Tests**—provide for a comprehensive assessment of selections included in a unit or in a specific literary period
- **Analogy Lessons**—give students an opportunity to practice analyzing the kinds of relationships that may be expressed in analogies
- **Analogy Tests**—help students gain proficiency in analyzing and solving analogy problems
- **Composition Tests**—offer a choice of writing prompts that call for the student to give a developed and thoughtful written response

TEACHER'S NOTES

UNIT 7: Modern Nonfiction

UNIT OBJECTIVES

The aims of this unit are for the student:

- To demonstrate an understanding of the basic nonfiction forms—essay, speech, and biography—and of the work of a number of outstanding modern nonfiction writers
- To identify and analyze White's use of gentle irony to show changes at Walden Pond and, by indirection, in American life
- To demonstrate an understanding of the relationship between society and the artist, including the artist's role and responsibilities, as expressed in an essay by Baldwin and a speech by Faulkner
- To identify the elements that led to a sense of place for Hinojosa-Smith and to explain the importance of place in his fiction
- To demonstrate an understanding of literary terms and techniques such as exaggeration, absurdity, sarcasm, mock-seriousness, repetition, and parallelism
- To analyze various selections by writing compositions or essays arguing against or in defense of one of Baldwin's statements and discussing Hurston's reading tastes

OVERVIEW OF THE UNIT

The introduction to this unit in the textbook discusses the various kinds of nonfiction forms represented by the selections. It should be noted that the unit contains prose pieces that stand as entities and those by Wright and Momaday, which are excerpted from longer works.

The material in this unit could also be approached thematically, for, as twentieth-century literature, it reflects contemporary issues: the relation of the modern artist to his or her society, the increasing pressures of urbanization and industrialization, and the special problems faced by minority groups in post-World War I America.

ANSWER KEYS

STUDY GUIDE

1. Essay, speech, and biography
2. The tone of an informal essay, as seen in the writings of E. B. White, can be humorous, personal, or relaxed.
3. It has an objective or serious tone, rigidly adheres to the rules of discourse, and is intended to instruct.
4. Literature or any of the arts
5. In autobiography, writers write about their own lives; in biography, authors write about the lives of others.
6. The former were eulogistic (written to extol the person's virtues) and were often dull.
7. Modern biographers concentrate on revealing incidents and on taking the liberty of entering a subject's mind. John Dos Passos, in his sketch of Henry Ford, uses these devices.

SELECTION TEST

1. b	3. d	5. a	7. d	9. a
2. d	4. b	6. b	8. b	10. b

Study Guide

MODERN NONFICTION

Introduction *(Page 865)*

1. List the three basic forms of nonfiction represented in this unit.

   _____

   _____

2. Characterize the tone of an informal essay and give an example of a writer who uses this form.

   _____

   _____

   _____

   _____

3. What are the characteristics of a formal essay?

   _____

   _____

   _____

   _____

4. What subjects does the critical essay deal with?

   _____

   _____

5. Explain the main difference between an autobiography and a biography.

   _____

   _____

   _____

   _____

   _____

   _____

continued ☞

6. In what ways are most biographies written in the nineteenth century different from those written by more recent biographers?

_____

_____

_____

7. List the two devices that twentieth-century biographers have borrowed from novelists. Give an example of an author who has used these methods.

_____

_____

_____

_____

_____

_____

Selection Test

MODERN NONFICTION

Introduction   *(Page 865)*

Directions: Write the letter of the *best* answer to each question. *(10 points each)*

1. The Introduction defines the essay as
   a. an elaborate, formal type of prose writing
   b. a relatively unrestricted yet organized type of prose writing
   c. any form of short prose that is factual
   d. any form of short, impersonal prose writing

   1. _____

2. The general purpose of the essay is mainly to
   a. entertain
   b. encourage thought
   c. amuse and distract
   d. both entertain and encourage thought

   2. _____

3. The tone of an informal essay can be any of the following *except*
   a. humorous
   b. personal
   c. relaxed
   d. scholarly

   3. _____

4. The aim of the formal essay is to
   a. amuse
   b. instruct
   c. debate
   d. inspire

   4. _____

5. The essay of E. B. White can be best described as
   a. informal
   b. formal
   c. both formal and informal
   d. impersonal and objective

   5. _____

6. Faulkner's speech was given on what kind of occasion?
   a. The launching of a space capsule
   b. The acceptance of an award
   c. The anniversary of a famous battle
   d. The inauguration of a president

   6. _____

7. In _____ (which includes autobiography), authors write about their own lives or the lives of _____.
   a. nonfiction . . . animals
   b. self-analysis . . . contemporaries
   c. memoirs . . . other writers
   d. biography . . . others

   7. _____

8. Modern biographers differ from nineteenth-century biographers in that modern ones are more
   a. scholarly
   b. candid
   c. flattering
   d. objective

   8. _____

continued ☞

9. Many biographers have come to regard themselves as _____
who _____, rather than record, facts.
   a. artists . . . interpret   **c.** journalists . . . research
   b. adapters . . . re-create   **d.** novelists . . . invent   **9.** _____

10. Some biographers who utilize certain literary techniques of the novelist
concentrate on _____ incidents and take the liberty of entering

_____.
   a. sordid . . . taboo subjects
   b. revealing . . . the subject's mind
   c. bizarre . . . a re-created realistic world
   d. fantasized . . . secret compartments of character   **10.** _____

TEACHER'S NOTES

WALDEN (JUNE 1939) *E. B. White* Text Page 866

OBJECTIVES

The aims of this lesson are for the student:
- To identify and analyze White's use of irony to express his attitudes toward the modern world
- To cite evidence given in White's essay that Walden has become less beautiful since Thoreau's era
- To analyze White's use of the letter format in his address to Thoreau

INTRODUCING THE SELECTION

After reviewing the biographical sketch in the textbook, you may tell the class that E. B. White was himself a man with a Thoreau-like preference for the rural over the urban. He expressed this preference by living on a farm in Maine even though his chief occupation was writing for *The New Yorker*. Away from the great city he could devote himself to writing, growing apples, and tending his livestock; he could "rediscover the charms of the old twisty roads . . . and barnyards with their mild congestions and pleasant smells."

Review the Thoreau selection on pages 232–243 before asking your class to read White. Tell the class that the new "Walden" which they are about to read is a typical personal essay. It does not try to overwhelm us with facts to prove a point, nor does it argue a thesis. It does not even ask us to believe anything. It merely recounts in an ironical and amiable fashion the author's own feelings as he tries to see the same Walden that Thoreau saw a century earlier.

SUMMARY

E. B. White uses the form of a letter to American naturalist Henry David Thoreau to make some amusing but caustic comparisons between twentieth-century life and the nineteenth-century time of Thoreau. In June of 1939, White drives to Concord to visit Walden Pond, where Thoreau lived and observed nature from 1845 to 1847. He tells Thoreau that the account of life at Walden Pond seems of more importance as "the world loses ground." White gives Thoreau a clear picture of the modern Concord environs—the highways, cars, and machines; the restaurant and trailer court near the woodland retreat; Thoreau's front yard marked by a bronze tablet set in stone; and the pond itself, now a State Preserve where people swim and boat. White says the total cost of his trip was what Thoreau spent for food for eight months.

READING/CRITICAL THINKING STRATEGIES

Finding Sequences

Before students begin their reading, you might ask them to discuss all the possible ways of organizing paragraphs: narration, description, definition, cause-and-effect, process, and so on. You may need to remind students that professional writers may use a variety of these modes when constructing an essay, while beginning writers often rely on only one or two modes. Tell students to consider the predominant mode of each paragraph in the essay. You may want to have them keep a chart like the one on page 7. After students have completed their reading, ask them to compare their findings and to discuss the overall aim and tone of the essay. Which parts of the essay speak most clearly to them? Why?

continued ☞

	Mode	Questions/Reactions
Paragraph 1	One sentence attention-getter	Why write a letter to a dead person?
Paragraph 2	Greeting/illustration	

VOCABULARY

The following words are defined in the glossary:

sojourn	(867)	harrow	(868)	intervene (–ing)	(869)
pertinence	(867)	cryptic	(868)	oasis	(870)
transcendental	(867)	distillation	(868)	congenial (ity)	(870)
stupefaction	(868)	inauspicious	(868)	petulant (ly)	(870)
imbibe (s)	(868)				

VOCABULARY ACTIVITY

In E. B. White's essay and the other nonfiction works that follow it in the textbook, students will encounter words that are unfamiliar to them. To help students tackle these words, provide the class with practice in analyzing word structure.

Ask students to choose ten words from the following list.

credibility
sojourn
pertinence
transcendental
stupefaction
imbibe
cryptic
immemorial
polytone
distillation
inauspicious
intervening
proprietor
congeniality
petulantly
undulated
extracted
contemptible

Tell students to write each word and then to divide it into its root and affix(es). Finally, have them create a definition for the word, based on the meaning of its root and affix(es) and on its context within the essay.

To ascertain how well students can apply their knowledge of roots and affixes, ask them to use the roots from five of their chosen words to create new words that have different meanings by adding different affixes. For example, the root of *intention* (line two in the third paragraph of White's essay) is *tendere;* other words formed from this root include *tend, pretend, intense, extend, tender, tendon, intend, attendant,* and *tendency.* You may wish to have students work in groups to complete this activity.

continued ☞

ANSWER KEYS

READING CHECK

A.
1. T
2. T
3. F

4. T
5. T

B. Answers will vary. Summaries should mention that White's comments are in the form of a letter to Thoreau. White's visit to Concord causes him to compare Thoreau's visit there with his own. He finds that modern society has left its mark, but that some things (the sound of a frog) have not changed. The letter ends with an accounting of expenses.

STUDY GUIDE

1. White refers to the writer as a gunner who must bring down "the bird of thought as it flashes by." Students' wording will vary.
2. Essays, stories, light verse, and children's books
3. Students' descriptions will vary, but may describe any of the following conveniences: the lawn mower, the car and its door locks, the trailer camp, and the facilities for swimmers at Walden Pond.

4. Some boys assembling the "framework of the rude shelter" were escaping from town, like Thoreau, to live naturally.
5. White describes the area around Concord as being "not quite suburban, not quite rural"; he notes the intensity of the church bells; he comments that Walden Pond is on Number 126, a state highway; he describes what remains of Thoreau's house—a bronze tablet and four granite posts; he describes the dressing rooms for swimmers at Walden Pond.
6. Definitions will vary.
7. **a.** Details about the menu point out the very ordinary nature of the lunchroom.
   b. The trailer people are crowded together and are abusing the natural setting—completely different from Thoreau's experience.
8. Paragraphs will vary.

BUILDING VOCABULARY

Answers will vary.

Reading Check

E. B. White   *Walden (June 1939)*   *(Page 867)*

─────────── READING CHECK ───────────

A.   True/False. Write T for a true statement. Write F for a false statement.

_____   **1.** Unlike Thoreau, E. B. White traveled to Walden Pond by automobile.

_____   **2.** The sign at the side of the road said that Route 62 had a cotton surface.

_____   **3.** White thought that Walden Breezes was a beautiful addition to the landscape.

_____   **4.** One of White's expenses on the trip was a baseball glove.

_____   **5.** The essay is written in the form of a letter to Henry David Thoreau.

B.   Write a summary of White's "Walden (June 1939)." As you write your summary, remember to

1. state ideas clearly and briefly,

2. state the topic of the essay,

3. include all main ideas (but do not include ideas not in the essay),

4. present the major ideas in the order in which they are given,

5. keep your summary to one or two brief paragraphs.

_____

_____

_____

_____

_____

_____

_____

_____

_____

_____

_____

_____

Study Guide

E. B. White (1899–1985)

WALDEN (June 1939) *(Pages 866–872)*

Understanding the Writer and His Background

1. According to E. B. White, a writer must be patient and quick. In your own words, identify the metaphor that White uses (in the introductory material for the selection) to explain his method.

   _____

   _____

   _____

2. What types or forms of writing did White use?

   _____

   _____

Understanding the Selection

3. E. B. White points out a number of ways that he and the people of Concord accomplish tasks that would be surprising to Thoreau. List three of the conveniences he mentions and briefly describe how White sees each being used.

   _____

   _____

   _____

4. Identify the group of human beings who, in White's view, are practicing Thoreau's philosophical spirit. How are their actions similar to those of Thoreau?

   _____

   _____

   _____

continued ☞

5. White's letter compares and contrasts his own observations of modern Concord and Walden Pond with the observations of Thoreau. What specific places does White describe, and how have they changed?

_____

_____

_____

_____

_____

_____

Understanding Vocabulary

6. The following words are taken from the selection. Using your textbook glossary or a dictionary, write a definition of each of the words.

sojourn _____

transcendental _____

contemptible _____

Understanding Literary Elements

7. E. B. White's humor lies in his use of "gentle irony," which seems to praise but really points out the shallowness of people. Listed below are two scenes described in the letter. Explain how White's use of details creates an ironic situation.

a. the lunchroom

_____

_____

_____

b. the trailer camp

_____

_____

_____

Writing and Responding to Literature

8. In the paragraph where White describes locking his car at night, he creates a humorous situation out of an ordinary task. He writes about a simple action in a way that makes it seem very complex. Rewrite this paragraph using a serious and objective tone. Use White's plan of organization by focusing on the how-to steps, but present the directions in a straightforward way.

_____

_____

_____

_____

_____

_____

_____

_____

_____

_____

_____

_____

_____

_____

_____

_____

_____

_____

E. B. White   *Walden (June 1939)*   *(Page 867)*

FINDING WORD ASSOCIATIONS

You can often remember the meanings of unfamiliar vocabulary words by relating the word or part of the word to a word you already know. For example, *sojourn,* which means "a brief stay or visit," has in it the beginning of the word *journey,* which means "a trip." Consequently, knowing the word *journey* can help you remember *sojourn.* While such devices may sometimes seem silly, they can be quite valuable in helping you to expand your vocabulary.

ACTIVITY

On the blanks provided, write association hints for ten of the words listed below from *Walden.* Use your dictionary to determine the meanings of words that are unfamiliar to you. Be prepared to share your hints with classmates.

pertinence	cryptic	oasis
stupefaction	distillation	congenial
imbibe	inauspicious	petulant
harrow	intervene	transcendental

1. _____

2. _____

3. _____

4. _____

5. _____

6. _____

7. _____

8. _____

9. _____

10. _____

TEACHER'S NOTES

THE CREATIVE PROCESS   *James Baldwin*   Text Page 873

OBJECTIVES

The aims of this lesson are for the student:
- To demonstrate an understanding of Baldwin's definition of an artist, including the artist's responsibilities, the relationship between the artist and society, and Baldwin's concept of "aloneness"
- To find synonyms for various words from the selection and to decide whether the synonyms clarify the meaning of Baldwin's sentences or make the meaning less precise
- To comment on initial reaction to selected works about artists from the public, critics, and government

INTRODUCING THE SELECTION

To the biographical introduction in the textbook you may add that James Baldwin, whose father was a New York clergyman from New Orleans, himself became a Pentecostal preacher when he was only fourteen. As he edited the literary magazine at DeWitt Clinton High School, he discovered that he would rather write than preach. Later, Richard Wright read a part of the manuscript for *Go Tell It on the Mountain* and encouraged Baldwin to continue. In his subsequent work, both fictional and nonfictional, Baldwin combined his earlier calling with his new role of writer.

SUMMARY

This critical essay presents Baldwin's views on the nature of the artist's responsibility to society. Baldwin says the artist must be at war with society because it is the artist's role to remind people of the universal, inescapable states of humanity—birth, suffering, love, and death. These frequently involve change, and people don't like their peace and traditions disturbed. They panic. The measure of maturity for nations and for people is their degree of preparedness to meet changes. The artist must be alone and try to better understand life. The artist must reveal all that is possible of the mystery of the human being. The artist must probe and take nothing for granted. American artists can improve the country's future by making people see the nation's historical record and understand clearly their strengths and weakness.

READING/CRITICAL THINKING STRATEGIES

Finding Main Ideas

As a prereading strategy, initiate a discussion of the creative process and the role of writers and other artists in society. How do students think that artists work? Why are artists important to a culture? Encourage students to discuss writers, painters, musicians, and so on whom they feel have made an important contribution to society. Tell students to pay close attention to what Baldwin says about the creative process and the role of artists. What main points does he make? Students might benefit from keeping a chart like the one below. After students have completed their reading, ask them to discuss their findings and to compare the ideas from their prereading discussion with Baldwin's ideas.

Paragraph	Main Idea
1	Unlike other human beings, the artist must work alone.
2	

continued ☞

VOCABULARY   The following words are defined in the glossary:

enjoin (ed)	**(874)**	**bulwark**	**(874)**	**belated**	**(875)**
extol (led)	**(874)**	**grandiloquent**	**(875)**	**ostracize**	**(875)**

ANSWER KEYS

READING CHECK

A. 1. T   4. F
2. T   5. T
3. F

B. Answers will vary. Students should mention that Baldwin discusses the role of the artist in society. The artist, he says, operates alone to show society a picture of itself that is not attractive. He explains that American society is particularly reluctant to look at itself as it really is.

STUDY GUIDE

1. To expose others to unpleasant realities, to "let us know that there is nothing stable under heaven," and to "drive to the heart of every answer and expose the question the answer hides"

2. *Go Tell It on the Mountain*—novel; *Notes of a Native Son*—collection of essays; *Nobody Knows My Name*—novel; *The Fire Next Time*—collection of essays; *Tell Me How Long the Train's Been Gone*—novel; *If Beale Street Could Talk*—novel; *The Price of the Ticket*—collection of essays.

3. 1) To cultivate the state of being alone; 2) to be an "incorrigible disturber of the peace"; and 3) to "reveal all that he can possibly discover concerning the mystery of the human being"

4. The artist seeks to create disturbances while society seeks to preserve order and tradition.

5. Because we as a nation have "modified and suppressed and lied" about our history, the American artist is trapped in his past, "immobilized in the prison of his undiscovered self."

6. Responses will vary.

LANGUAGE SKILLS

A. 1. whom   7. who
2. who   8. Whom
3. who   9. Who
4. who   10. Who
5. whom   11. whom
6. who   12. Who

B. 13. The teacher is looking for a student who is interested in entering the essay contest.
14. Four students whom the teacher asked said they want to write essays about artists.
15. Contestants who submit a rough draft will be given the rules for a final version.

BUILDING VOCABULARY

Answers will vary.

SELECTION TEST

1. b   4. b
2. a   5. b
3. c

NAME _____

CLASS _____ DATE _____ SCORE _____

James Baldwin   *The Creative Process*   (Page 874)

―――――――――――――――― **READING CHECK** ――――――――――――――――

A. **True/False.** Write T for a true statement. Write F for a false statement.

_____ 1. According to Baldwin, the artist must cultivate the state of being alone.

_____ 2. Baldwin says that society has always battled the artist.

_____ 3. Future societies, according to Baldwin, will get along better with the artist.

_____ 4. Baldwin says that it is the artist's duty to preserve order and tradition.

_____ 5. Baldwin calls the artist's war with society a lover's war.

B. Write a summary of Baldwin's essay. As you write your summary, remember to

1. state ideas clearly and briefly,

2. state the topic of the essay,

3. include all main ideas (but do not include ideas not in the essay),

4. present the major ideas in the order in which they are given,

5. keep your summary to one or two brief paragraphs.

_____

_____

_____

_____

_____

_____

_____

_____

_____

_____

_____

Study Guide

James Baldwin (1924–1987)

THE CREATIVE PROCESS   *(Pages 873–876)*

Understanding the Writer and His Background

1. What is Baldwin's duty as an artist, as he sees it? _____

_____

_____

_____

2. List three of Baldwin's published works and beside each indicate whether it is a novel or a collection of essays.

_____

_____

_____

_____

Understanding the Selection

3. List at least three things that Baldwin says are the duties of the artist if he or she is to

be creative. _____

_____

_____

_____

4. Explain why Baldwin believes society views the artist as the "disturber of the peace."*

_____

_____

_____

_____

*Excerpts appearing in this Study Guide are from "The Creative Process" from *Creative America* by James Baldwin. Published by Ridge Press. Collected in *The Price of the Ticket* (St. Martin's Press, 1985). Reprinted by permission of the **James Baldwin Estate**.

continued ☞

5. According to Baldwin, how are the problems of the American artist different from those of artists elsewhere?

_____

_____

_____

_____

_____

Writing and Responding to Literature

6. Baldwin writes that there is, and must be, a warlike relationship existing between the artist and society. In a few sentences, indicate whether or not you agree with Baldwin and explain why you feel as you do.

_____

_____

_____

_____

_____

_____

_____

_____

_____

Language Skills

The Creative Process   *James Baldwin*   *(Page 874)*

WHO AND *WHOM*

When writers use *who* and *whom* as relative pronouns introducing subordinate clauses, the form they choose depends on how the pronoun functions in the clause. As you read the following excerpt, notice how James Baldwin distinguishes between *who* and *whom*.

> The human beings <u>whom</u> we respect the most, after all—and sometimes fear the most—are those <u>who</u> are deeply involved in this delicate and strenuous effort. . . . That nation is healthiest which has the least necessity to distrust or ostracize or victimize these people—<u>whom</u>, as I say, we honor, once they are gone. . . .   *(Page 875)*

Who is the nominative case form, and *whom* is the objective case form. If the pronoun functions as a subject or a predicate nominative, *who* is correct.

EXAMPLES   <u>who</u> are deeply involved   **[Subject; nominative case]**

The artist is <u>who</u> Baldwin thinks   **[Predicate nominative; nominative case]**
lights the darkness.

If the pronoun functions as an object, *whom* is correct. When *who* and *whom* are used as **interrogative pronouns,** to ask a question, the same rules apply.

EXAMPLES   <u>whom</u> we respect the most   **[Direct object of the verb *respect*; objective case]**

The friend with <u>whom</u> I usually   **[Object of the preposition *with*; objective case]**
study has a cold.

EXAMPLES   **NOMINATIVE**

<u>Who</u> wrote the essay?   **[*Who* is the subject of the verb *wrote*.]**

<u>Who</u> should it be?   **[*Who* is a predicate nominative.]**

EXAMPLES   **OBJECTIVE**

<u>Whom</u> did you ask?   **[*Whom* is the direct object of the verb *did ask*.]**

With <u>whom</u> do you usually study?   **[*Whom* is the object of the preposition *with*.]**

Excerpts appearing in this Language Skills worksheet are from "The Creative Process" from *Creative America* by James Baldwin. Published by Ridge Press. Collected in *The Price of the Ticket* (St. Martin's Press, 1985). Reprinted by permission of the *James Baldwin Estate*.

continued ☞

ACTIVITY A

In the blank provided, complete each of the following sentences with the correct form: *who* or *whom*.

1. Baldwin says we should not make life difficult for our artists, _____ we honor once they are dead.

2. Baldwin defines artists as people _____ actively seek to be alone.

3. Most of us are busy with public matters; the artist is a person _____ examines the mysteries of life.

4. Baldwin compares the artist's aloneness with that of a person _____ is suffering.

5. Artists are those to _____ we turn with questions about society's traditions and delusions.

6. Baldwin says that those _____ understand themselves do less damage to themselves and others.

7. Baldwin urges those _____ say that they live in the "New World" to ask what they mean by that term.

8. _____ did Baldwin meet while he was working on his first novel?

9. _____ wrote *The Price of the Ticket?*

10. _____, according to Baldwin, has the task of cultivating aloneness?

11. In the war with society, with _____ does Baldwin compare the artist?

12. _____, in Baldwin's opinion, has an opportunity unique in history?

continued ☞

ACTIVITY B

Combine each of the following pairs of sentences by using *who* or *whom* to make the second sentence a subordinate clause.

EXAMPLE   I know the girl.
          You invited the girl.

I know the girl whom you invited. _____

13. The teacher is looking for a student.
    That student is interested in entering the essay contest.

    _____

    _____

14. Four students said they want to write essays about artists.
    The teacher asked four students.

    _____

    _____

15. Contestants will be given the rules for a final version.
    Contestants submit a rough draft.

    _____

    _____

NAME _____

CLASS _____ DATE _____ SCORE _____

James Baldwin   *The Creative Process*   *(Page 874)*

────────────────── **USING CONTEXT CLUES** ──────────────────

ACTIVITY

The italicized word in each of the following sentences is used by James Baldwin in "The Creative Process." As directed, give an example of the word based on your own experience.

1. Baldwin says that he may be making *grandiloquent* claims for the role of the artist in our society. Describe a television commercial that you have seen or a speech that you have heard in which someone made grandiloquent claims.

_____

_____

_____

_____

2. In "The Creative Process," Baldwin writes that the fact that humans are essentially alone is a *banality*. Name a statement that you have heard many times that you feel is a banality.

_____

_____

_____

_____

3. According to Baldwin, the artist is "an *incorrigible* disturber of the peace." Briefly describe the imaginary history of a criminal whom a judge has called incorrigible.

_____

_____

_____

_____

Excerpts appearing in this Building Vocabulary worksheet are from "The Creative Process" from *Creative America* by James Baldwin. Published by Ridge Press. Collected in *The Price of the Ticket* (St. Martin's Press, 1985). Reprinted by permission of the **James Baldwin Estate**.

continued ☞

4. Baldwin says that it is *inevitable* that people will not want to make changes in traditions. Based on your reading of American history, do you feel that it was inevitable that the American colonies would declare their independence from Britain? Why?

_____

_____

_____

_____

5. Baldwin feels that humans are *enjoined* to come to terms with themselves. Briefly describe something that you feel the United States as a nation is enjoined at this time to do.

_____

_____

_____

_____

6. Love, according to Baldwin, is a force that many have *extolled*. Name three things that you have heard extolled recently.

_____

_____

_____

_____

7. Society, says Baldwin, gives its artists *belated* honor. Describe a situation in which your state government or our national government has paid belated honor to someone in a formal way.

_____

_____

_____

_____

E. B. White *and* James Baldwin

AN OPEN-BOOK TEST   *(Pages 866–876)*

Directions: Write the letter of the best answer to each question. (*10 points each*)

1. In "Walden (June 1939)," E. B. White is reminded of the spirit of Thoreau when he sees
   a. people staying at the trailer park
   b. a group of boys building a playhouse
   c. the swimmers in Walden Pond
   d. the owners of the Golden Pheasant   1. _____

2. What does White mean when he says that Thoreau's *Walden* each year "seems to gain a little headway, as the world loses ground"?
   a. That it grows in meaning
   b. That it becomes less important
   c. That it seems more and more trivial
   d. That it becomes more complicated   2. _____

3. In the first paragraph of his essay on the creative process, Baldwin states that the "precise role of the artist" is to
   a. isolate himself from society
   b. live a different life from the ordinary person
   c. make the world a better place in which to live
   d. write Pulitzer Prize-winning books   3. _____

4. Baldwin defines the artist's role in relation to society as a(n)
   a. keeper of the peace
   b. incorrigible disturber of the peace
   c. goldfish among barracuda
   d. prince among swine   4. _____

5. According to Baldwin, artists should be more responsible to
   a. themselves   c. posterity
   b. society   d. art   5. _____

TEACHER'S NOTES

NOBEL PRIZE ACCEPTANCE SPEECH
William Faulkner

Text Page 877

OBJECTIVES

The aims of this lesson are for the student:
- To identify rhetorical devices such as repetition and parallelism in Faulkner's speech
- To identify and interpret Faulkner's positive outlook for humanity and his views on the writer's role in society
- To write an essay based on research about the Nobel prize

INTRODUCING THE SELECTION

The class might be interested in knowing something about the Nobel Prize for literature awarded to William Faulkner on December 10, 1950. Its founder, Alfred Nobel (1833–1896), a wealthy Swedish inventor and manufacturer, believed that literature should have humanitarian goals, and stipulated in his will that one of the five annual prizes he had endowed should be awarded to the person "who shall have produced in the field of literature the most outstanding work of an idealistic tendency." Like Baldwin's essay, Faulkner's speech delineates the role of the artist in society. You could ask the class to compare and contrast the treatment of this theme in the two works.

SUMMARY

In his acceptance speech for the Nobel Prize in 1950, Faulkner advises young writers on their proper role in society. He says that modern writers have been worried over the possibility of being blown up and have forgotten what makes for good writing and is the only thing worth writing about—"the problems of the human heart in conflict with itself." Writers must not be afraid and must learn this so that they can be concerned with the universal truths of love, honor, pity, pride, compassion, and sacrifice. He ends by declaring his faith in humankind: "I believe that man will not merely endure: he will prevail."

READING/CRITICAL THINKING STRATEGIES

Expressing an Opinion

Before students begin their reading, you might ask them to discuss what they think is worth writing and reading about. You might encourage them to consider what they think "the human heart in conflict with itself" might mean. Tell students to pay careful attention to Faulkner's views of the roles of the writer and of literature. You might encourage students to keep a chart like the one below. After students have completed their reading, ask them to share their findings and to consider whether they agree or disagree with all or some of Faulkner's ideas. If students have read James Baldwin's "The Creative Process," you might ask them to compare or contrast Faulkner's views with Baldwin's.

Faulkner's Major Claims	Questions/Reactions
The writer's role is to create something new out of the human spirit.	How do writers create material? What does the creative process involve?

continued ☞

VOCABULARY The following words are defined in the glossary:

commensurate (877)	verity (–ies) (877)	ephemeral (877)
pinnacle (877)		

ANSWER KEYS

READING CHECK

Nobel Prize Acceptance Speech   Text Page 877

A. 1. T   4. F
   2. F   5. T
   3. F

B. Answers will vary. Students should mention the occasion of the speech, that Faulkner describes the duties of the writer in the modern age, and that those duties include reminding people of their compassionate spirit.

STUDY GUIDE

Nobel Prize Acceptance Speech   Text Page 877

1. Oppressive, violent themes; use of classical mythology and Faulkner's private mythology; extremely complex structure and language

2. His technical virtuosity; his works' thematic richness; his great expressiveness; his remarkable range of character, situations, and tones

3. The problems of the human heart in conflict with itself

4. Because a person has a soul, "a spirit capable of compassion and sacrifice and endurance," he or she is immortal

5. Paragraphs will vary.

BUILDING VOCABULARY

Nobel Prize Acceptance Speech   Text Page 877

A. **Humanity Prevails**   **Opposing Forces**
   verity   anguish
   inexhaustible   timidity
   endure   cowardice
   compassion   annihilate
   fortitude   ravage
   triumph   despairing
   resolute   nihility
   tenacious

B. Responses will vary.

SELECTION VOCABULARY TEST

James Baldwin   Text Page 873
William Faulkner   Text Page 877

1. g   3. f   5. a   7. e   9. b
2. c   4. d   6. j   8. i   10. h

Reading Check

William Faulkner   *Nobel Prize Acceptance Speech*   *(Page 877)*

─────────────────────── **READING CHECK** ───────────────────────

A.   True/False. Write T for a true statement. Write F for a false statement.

_____ **1.** Faulkner states his writing is concerned with the human spirit.

_____ **2.** He says that fear of atomic destruction has created new opportunities for literary expression.

_____ **3.** Faulkner argues that literature has dealt with old subjects long enough and must now turn to new subjects.

_____ **4.** Faulkner praises the writers' capacity to be afraid.

_____ **5.** He states that humanity will not only endure but will prevail.

B.   Write a summary of Faulkner's speech. As you write your summary, remember to

1. state ideas clearly and briefly,

2. state the topic of the speech,

3. include all main ideas (but do not include ideas not in the speech),

4. present the major ideas in the order in which they are given,

5. keep your summary to one or two brief paragraphs.

_____

_____

_____

_____

_____

_____

_____

_____

_____

Study Guide

William Faulkner (1897–1962)

NOBEL PRIZE ACCEPTANCE SPEECH   *(Pages 877–878)*

Understanding the Writer and His Background

1. Identify two characteristics of Faulkner's writing that caused him to be regarded merely as an eccentric regional writer by critics of the 1930s and 1940s.

   _____

   _____

   _____

2. Later, in the late 1940s, critics Malcolm Cowley and Robert Penn Warren found characteristics worthy of praise in Faulkner's work, and he began to receive critical acclaim. Identify at least two characteristics of his work that received critical acclaim.

   _____

   _____

   _____

   _____

Understanding the Selection

3. According to Faulkner, what type of problem is worthy of the writer's consideration, or "worth writing about"?

   _____

   _____

4. What characteristic, in Faulkner's view, makes human beings "immortal"?

   _____

   _____

   _____

continued ☞

Writing and Responding to Literature

5. In his acceptance speech, Faulkner spoke not to the general population of the world but to those people who were, or were planning to become, writers. Do you think it was appropriate for him to limit his acceptance speech to a particular group of people? Write a brief paragraph explaining why you think his choice of a limited audience was or was not appropriate.

_____

_____

_____

_____

_____

_____

_____

_____

_____

_____

_____

_____

_____

_____

Building Vocabulary

William Faulkner *Nobel Prize Acceptance Speech* (Page 877)

———— CLASSIFYING WORD CONNOTATIONS / USING WORDS IN CONTEXT ————

In his Nobel Prize Acceptance Speech, William Faulkner uses many words with strong positive connotations, such as *pinnacle,* to describe the capacity of the human spirit to prevail. He also uses words with negative connotaions, such as *ephemeral,* to describe forces that humanity must overcome in order to prevail.

ACTIVITY A

Below is a list of words that can describe the human spirit's struggle to overcome opposing forces. Use the connotation of each word to decide whether it belongs under the heading *Humanity Prevails* or *Opposing Forces,* and then write it under that heading.

verity	inexhaustible	compassion	ravage	nihility
anguish	cowardice	annihilate	triumph	resolute
timidity	endure	fortitude	despairing	tenacious

Humanity Prevails   **Opposing Forces**

_____   _____

_____   _____

_____   _____

_____   _____

_____   _____

_____   _____

_____   _____

_____   _____

_____   _____

continued ☞

ACTIVITY B

If Faulkner were alive today, how do you think he would respond to the question "Has humanity prevailed?" In the space provided, write your response to that question. In doing so, use at least three of the following words: *commensurate, pinnacle, verity, ephemeral.*

_____

_____

_____

_____

_____

_____

_____

_____

_____

_____

_____

_____

_____

_____

_____

_____

_____

_____

_____

NAME _____

CLASS _____ DATE _____ SCORE _____

James Baldwin
William Faulkner

The Creative Process   *(Page 874)*
Nobel Prize Acceptance Speech   *(Page 877)*

─────────── **VOCABULARY TEST** ───────────

Directions: Match each word in column I with the correct definition in column II. Place the letter of each definition you choose in the space provided. (7 points each)

I	II
_____ 1. enjoin	**a.** late
_____ 2. extol	**b.** truth
_____ 3. bulwark	**c.** to praise
_____ 4. grandiloquent	**d.** grandiose; high-flown
_____ 5. belated	**e.** equal to
_____ 6. ostracize	**f.** a strong defense
_____ 7. commensurate	**g.** to command
_____ 8. pinnacle	**h.** short-lived
_____ 9. verity	**i.** a culmination or high point
_____ 10. ephemeral	**j.** to reject or exclude

TEACHER'S NOTES

THIS WRITER'S SENSE OF PLACE

Rolando R. Hinojosa-Smith

Text Page 879

OBJECTIVES

The aims of this lesson are for the student:
- To identify the elements that led to a sense of place for Hinojosa-Smith, and to explain the importance of place in his fiction
- To explain why Hinojosa-Smith does not feel "limited" by writing about a small area in Texas
- To cite and explain the literary techniques Hinojosa-Smith uses in presenting the conflicts of culture and language on the Border
- To write several paragraphs about an incident from the student's past, steeping the incident in the particulars of the place in which the student was raised

INTRODUCING THE SELECTION

Born and raised in a small Rio Grande Valley border town of South Texas, Hinojosa-Smith, from his earliest days, was steeped in the rich tradition of his family, his forebears, and the Chicano heritage and culture. Hundreds of characters, all an integral part of the "community" of the Border, emerge from his Klail City, Belken County novels. A unique ability to unify past, present, and future generations of this area is dramatized repeatedly in all of his works.

Hinojosa-Smith's conviction that his main function as a writer is to concentrate on sense of place resulted in his first, and probably most important, novel, *Estampas del Valle y Otras Obras,* later translated and published in English as *The Valley.* This work reveals in vivid detail the people and locale of the author's early experiences through semi-autobiographical narrative voices like those of Jehú Malacara and Rafe Buenrostro. These same characters and a kaleidoscope of others reappear in several other novels (*Rites and Witnesses, Dear Rafe,* and *Partners in Crime,* a Rafe Buenrostro mystery).

The body of American literature is a testimonial to writers who, like Hinojosa-Smith, have worked ardently to develop a "sense" of America and its people. From the chronicles of early colonists like Bradford to the masterpieces of the nineteenth- and twentieth-century "greats" like Hawthorne, Twain, Cather, Steinbeck, Faulkner, and Ellison, the narratives of American authors present the diversity of geographical places, people, and cultures represented in our vast land. To this august group of American writers, authors like Hinojosa-Smith are currently making major contributions.

SUMMARY

The importance of place—specifically, the Rio Grande Valley in South Texas along the Texas-Mexico border—to his writings is discussed in this speech by Hinojosa-Smith at a conference on the Texas literary tradition. For him, as for many other authors, writing about his place of origin and upbringing became essential. It gave him the subjects and people about which to write—the Chicano culture of the Border. He admires writers who express a love and understanding of a particular place. He traces his own sense of place to growing up in the Valley and hearing the stories of its people. The border wasn't paradise, he notes, but it was home. Its people were unified by their past, a strong oral history, their names, and language. He left the Valley but found direction in his writing by going back to the Spanish language and the Border setting.

Excerpts appearing in the Teacher's Notes for Rolando Hinojosa-Smith are from "This Writer's Sense of Place" by R. R. Hinojosa-Smith from *The Texas Literary Tradition,* edited by Don Graham, James W. Lee, and William T. Pilkington. Published by The University of Texas at Austin, 1983. Reprinted by permission of **R. R. Hinojosa-Smith.**

continued ☞

Differentiating Fact and Opinion

As a prereading strategy, ask students what they think is meant by the phrase *a sense of place*. Encourage students to discuss literature and films in which a sense of place plays an important role. Do students consider a sense of place important in literature and film? Is it important in real life? Tell students to think about why the author considers a sense of place important in literature. What facts and opinions does the author use to support his thesis? Students might benefit from keeping a chart like the one below. After students have finished their reading, ask them to compare their findings and to discuss whether or not they agree with the author. Encourage students to support their opinions with fact.

Statements of Fact	Statements of Opinion	Mixture of Fact and Opinion
Navarro was imprisoned.		
Navarro signed Declaration of Independence.		

VOCABULARY

The following words are defined in the glossary:

extol (ling)	(880)	unwary	(881)	foster (ed)	(883)
apocryphal	(880)	exploit (s)	(882)	impart	(884)
jurisdictional	(881)	denigrate	(882)	mythicize	(884)
promulgate (d)	(881)	exorbitant	(882)	persona	(884)
propagate (d)	(881)	interloper (s)	(882)	milieu	(884)
pejorative	(881)	indigenous	(882)	anthropology	(884)
imbibe (d)	(881)	stultify (–ied)	(883)	fidelity	(885)
eschew	(881)	inoperative	(883)		

ANSWER KEYS

STUDY GUIDE

This Writer's Sense of Place   Text Page 879

1. The ways in which members of the Rio Grande Chicano culture cope with the larger American world
2. The Rio Grande Valley
3. The people, the culture and history, names, and language
4. The people who "populate" the stories hold them together.
5. The writer's having "fidelity to history"

6. Sentences will vary.
7. Paragraphs will vary.

LANGUAGE SKILLS

This Writer's Sense of Place   Text Page 879

A. 1. named; names
   2. home; home
   3. Mexico; Mexico
   4. Texas-Mexicans; Mexican
   5. the place and its history; a place, its history

continued ☞

6. on the Border, in the Valley; that space

B. 7.–10. Answers will vary.

B. 1. g	**4.** a
2. e	**5.** d
3. h	

BUILDING VOCABULARY

This Writer's Sense of Place   Text Page 879

1. b	**6.** a
2. b	**7.** a
3. b	**8.** b
4. b	**9.** a
5. a	**10.** b

SELECTION VOCABULARY TEST

This Writer's Sense of Place   Text Page 879

A.	**1.** c	**9.** c
	2. b	**10.** a
	3. a	**11.** c
	4. c	**12.** a
	5. a	**13.** c
	6. a	**14.** d
	7. d	**15.** a
	8. a	

SELECTION TEST

William Faulkner   Text Page 877
Rolando R. Hinojosa-Smith   Text Page 879

1. b	**4.** b
2. c	**5.** a
3. d	

NAME _____

CLASS _____ DATE _____ SCORE _____

Rolando R. Hinojosa-Smith (1929–   )

THIS WRITER'S SENSE OF PLACE *(Pages 879–885)*

Understanding the Writer and His Background

1. What does Hinojosa-Smith's work depict about Chicano culture? In other words, what is the central concern, or theme, of his work?

_____

_____

_____

Understanding the Selection

2. What geographical place does Hinojosa-Smith write about?

_____

3. According to Hinojosa-Smith, his sense of place is more than a geographical location. List three important elements, other than geography, that are necessary to his reconstruction of a sense of place.

_____

_____

4. Hinojosa-Smith writes that his stories are not "held together by . . . the plot." What does he feel holds them together?

_____

_____

5. What does Hinojosa-Smith think is "the first step to fixing a sense of place"?

_____

_____

Excerpts appearing in this Study Guide are from "This Writer's Sense of Place" by R. R. Hinojosa-Smith from *The Texas Literary Tradition,* edited by Don Graham, James W. Lee, and William T. Pilkington. Published by The University of Texas at Austin, 1983. Reprinted by permission of *R. R. Hinojosa-Smith*.

continued ☞

Understanding Vocabulary

6. The following words are used by Hinojosa-Smith in "This Writer's Sense of Place." Use the glossary in the textbook or a dictionary to determine the meaning of each word. Then write a sentence using the word.

promulgate(d) _____

_____

_____

denigrate _____

_____

_____

indigenous _____

_____

milieu _____

_____

_____

fidelity _____

_____

_____

continued ☞

Writing and Responding to Literature

7. Rolando R. Hinojosa-Smith writes of the importance of geographical place, history, names, and language in the development of a sense of place. Think about the writing of two or three of your favorite authors. Is a sense of place important in their writing? Are their stories or books always set in the same geographical area with the same types of people? On the basis of your discoveries about other writers whose stories you enjoy, write a paragraph or two agreeing or disagreeing with Hinojosa-Smith's opinion of the importance of a sense of place.

_____

_____

_____

_____

_____

_____

_____

_____

_____

_____

_____

_____

_____

_____

_____

_____

_____

_____

_____

Language Skills

This Writer's Sense of Place
Rolando R. Hinojosa-Smith   *(Page 879)*

─────────── **CONNECTIONS BETWEEN PARAGRAPHS** ───────────

To establish a smooth and logical flow of ideas throughout an essay, writers connect ideas from paragraph to paragraph. As you read the following excerpt, notice how Rolando Hinojosa-Smith effectively links two paragraphs.

> As you may already know, it's no accident that Jim Wells County in South Texas is named for him.   **[Last sentence of paragraph]**
>
> One of the earliest stories I heard about Grandfather Smith was a supposed conversation he had with Lawyer Wells. . . .   **[First sentence of new paragraph]**
> *(Page 880)*

Hinojosa-Smith links the idea in the second of the two paragraphs to the idea in the preceding paragraph by mentioning Wells again. Such **direct references** to a preceding idea can be made by repeating words and phrases or by using pronouns or synonyms.

ACTIVITY A

The following quotations are the last and first sentences of consecutive paragraphs. Circle the words that connect the two sentences in each pair.

1. . . . it was Nuevo Santander, named for old Santander in the Spanish Peninsula.
    The last names were similar up and down on both banks of the river. . . .
    (Page 881)

2. . . . (as Frost once wrote) home, when you have to go there, is the place where they have to take you in.
    And the Border was home. . . .   *(Page 881)*

3. . . . they bided their time to return to Mexico.
    But we didn't return to Mexico. . . .   *(Page 882)*

4. . . . the price that many Texas-Mexicans paid for keeping the language and the sense of place has been exorbitant.
    As a Borderer, the northbank Mexican couldn't . . . "go back to where you came from."   *(Page 882)*

Excerpts appearing in this Language Skills worksheet are from "This Writer's Sense of Place" by R. R. Hinojosa-Smith from *The Texas Literary Tradition,* edited by Don Graham, James W. Lee, and William T. Pilkington. Published by The University of Texas at Austin, 1983. Reprinted by permission of *R. R. Hinojosa-Smith.*

continued ☞

5. ... values ... were fashioned and forged by the place and its history.
What I am saying here is not ... that it is impossible for a writer to write about a place, its history. ...   *(Page 883)*

6. ... I decided to set it on the Border, in the Valley.
As reduced as that space was, it too was Texas. ...   *(Page 884)*

ACTIVITY B

Read each of the following paragraphs. Then write an opening sentence for a paragraph that could follow the one here.

7.   One reason I prefer cats to dogs is that they are more independent. I can leave them for a weekend with their food and water dishes full, and they will eat only when they are hungry. A dog would gobble its food as soon as the door closed behind me— and starve the rest of the weekend. Being able to leave cats for more than one day isn't the only advantage, however.

_____

_____

8.   Another value important to me is honesty. I always try to be honest with others and myself, and I expect others to be honest with me. It's simply easier not to lie or cheat or avoid difficult issues. Remembering what excuse I gave someone for not going to a party is too complicated.

_____

_____

9.   I don't enjoy going to movies. I always end up behind someone who is bushy-haired or extraordinarily tall. After an hour or so, my neck hurts from trying to look around the obstacle in front of me, and my back hurts from the uncomfortable seat, and my popcorn is gone before the movie is half over. Physical discomforts are not my only objections to movies, however.

_____

_____

10.   A word processor has many useful features. One of these is that you can see, as you write, how your draft would appear printed. One glance at the screen allows you to plan your spacing, notice words that you have used too many times, and catch typographical errors. Seeing these mistakes quickly and easily is only one of the miracles of a word processor.

_____

_____

Rolando R. Hinojosa-Smith   *This Writer's Sense of Place*   (Page 879)

USING CONTEXT TO DETERMINE MEANING

The words that surround a particular word in a sentence or paragraph are called the **context** of that word. In many cases, the context of a word can provide clues about that word's meaning. For example, consider the following sentence in which context clues provide hints about the meaning of the word *nocturnal*.

> Soon after sundown, the nocturnal creatures of the desert begin to stir and venture out of their dens and nests.

In this example, the phrases "Soon after sundown" and "venture out of their dens and nests" indicate that the "nocturnal creatures of the desert" become active after dark. Consequently, these clues reveal that the word *nocturnal* means "active during the nighttime."

ACTIVITY

Each of the italicized words in the following sentences is from "This Writer's Sense of Place." For each word, two definitions are given. Using the context of the sentence, identify which of the definitions is correct. (Note: The word *gringo* is italicized in two sentences because it is a foreign word; find the other italicized word in those sentences and identify its definition.)

_____ 1. It was the *gringos*, according to Rolando Hinojosa-Smith, who assumed that the term *"gringo"* was a *pejorative* label.
   a. declining   **b.** downgrading

_____ 2.   The fact that second and third cousins were allowed to marry *promulgated* a sense of belonging among Borderers.
   a. made known officially   **b.** made publicly known

_____ 3. The Borderers lived along the banks of the Rio Grande long before the *gringos, interlopers* from the North, began coming.
   a. unauthorized traders   **b.** intruders

_____ 4. Rolando Hinojosa-Smith believes that writers such as Larry McMurtry *impart* a sense of place in many of their works.
   a. give a share of   **b.** bestow

_____ 5. As one grows up, Hinojosa-Smith writes, one may adopt a *persona* with which to face the outer world.
   a. outer personality, or mask   **b.** character in a novel or drama

continued ☞

_____ **6.** Hinojosa-Smith says that his purpose is not to *denigrate* the formula novel, that he considers it fine art, if done well.
a. defame **b.** blacken

_____ **7.** Hinojosa-Smith says that "*fidelity* to history is the first step to fixing a sense of place."
a. accuracy, as of a description or translation **b.** loyalty as to a vow

_____ **8.** The fact that the phrase "go back to where you came from" was "inoperative" for them helped to *foster* a sense of place among the Border Mexicans.
a. adopt **b.** promote

_____ **9.** As he grew up, Hinojosa-Smith was *steeped* in the exploits of Juan Nepomuceno Cortina.
a. immersed **b.** soaked in liquid

_____ **10.** Hinojosa-Smith says that his attitude toward writers such as Philip Roth, who impart a sense of place in their works, is not a *studied* opinion; it arises, rather, from a certain love for the place.
a. well-informed **b.** premeditated

NAME _____

CLASS _____ DATE _____ SCORE _____

Rolando R. Hinojosa-Smith *This Writer's Sense of Place*   (Page 879)

──────────────────────── **VOCABULARY TEST** ────────────────────────

A. Write the letter of the *best* synonym for each word. (5 points each)

_____ **1. extol** (a) separate (b) add (c) praise (d) punish

_____ **2. indigenous** (a) angry (b) native (c) mosaic (d) crafty

_____ **3. promulgate** (a) publicize (b) chastise (c) change (d) hide

_____ **4. denigrate** (a) gratify (b) scratch (c) defame (d) praise

_____ **5. imbibe** (a) absorb (b) read (c) drink (d) dig

_____ **6. eschew** (a) avoid (b) revert (c) admit (d) greet

_____ **7. interloper** (a) runner (b) thread (c) guest (d) intruder

_____ **8. apocryphal** (a) fictitious (b) ancient (c) trustworthy (d) foreign

_____ **9. pejorative** (a) prejudiced (b) false (c) downgrading (d) elaborate

_____ **10. propagate** (a) multiply (b) publish (c) sidestep (d) diminish

_____ **11. exorbitant** (a) circular (b) fraudulent (c) extravagant (d) small

_____ **12. foster** (a) promote (b) substitute (c) discourage (d) defraud

_____ **13. milieu** (a) thousands (b) countless (c) surroundings (d) arsenal

_____ **14. fidelity** (a) fortune (b) reverence (c) hate (d) faithfulness

_____ **15. impart** (a) give (b) divide (c) receive (d) promote

B. Match each numbered definition with a word from the list below. Place the letter of each word you choose in the space provided. (5 points each)

a. jurisdictional   **d.** exploit   **g.** stultify
b. inoperative   **e.** anthropology   **h.** unwary
c. mythicize   **f.** persona

_____ **1.** To make dull

_____ **2.** Study of development and behavior of human beings

_____ **3.** Unguarded

_____ **4.** Having to do with the territorial extent of authority

_____ **5.** Bold or brilliant deed

NAME _____

CLASS _____ DATE _____ SCORE _____

William Faulkner *and* Rolando R. Hinojosa-Smith

AN OPEN-BOOK TEST   *(Pages 877–885)*

Directions: Write the letter of the *best* answer to each question. *(10 points each)*

1. In his Nobel Prize acceptance speech, Faulkner says the writer is basically a
   a. historian   **c.** public servant
   b. creator   **d.** lonely, misunderstood creature   **1.** _____

2. Which one of the following was Faulkner *least* interested in?
   a. Fame   **c.** Profit
   b. Credibility   **d.** Immortality   **2.** _____

3. The main portion of Faulkner's speech is addressed to
   a. his readers   **c.** future generations
   b. the Swedish people   **d.** young writers   **3.** _____

4. Hinojosa-Smith gets his "sense of place" from all of the following *except* the
   a. language used   **c.** values held
   b. Border disputes   **d.** historical associations   **4.** _____

5. According to Saldívar, having a sense of place allowed Hinojosa-Smith to
   ignore which of the following in his novel *The Valley*?
   a. Strict chronology   **c.** Plot
   b. Texas history   **d.** Social customs   **5.** _____

Excerpts appearing in this Selection Test are from "This Writer's Sense of Place" by R. R. Hinojosa-Smith from *The Texas Literary Tradition,* edited by Don Graham, James W. Lee, and William T. Pilkington. Published by The University of Texas at Austin, 1983. Reprinted by permission of **R. R. Hinojosa-Smith**.

TEACHER'S NOTES

NOBEL LECTURE IN LITERATURE

Toni Morrison Text Page 888

OBJECTIVES

The aims of this lesson are for the student:
- To identify the analogy of old woman/bird and writer/language
- To identify Morrison's attitude about language and its use
- To express a personal opinion about the significance of language

INTRODUCING THE SELECTION

Toni Morrison, the first African American woman to win the coveted Nobel Prize for literature, is a novelist and editor. Within her well-crafted fiction, usually about young African American women facing racism and sexism, Morrison often uses literary devices such as symbolism, foreshadowing, and flashbacks. Skilled at characterization, she compresses dialogue so tightly that her characters' authentic dialect sparkles.

SUMMARY

In her lecture, Toni Morrison relays a story about children and an elderly, wise, blind woman. One of the children asks her if the bird the child is holding is alive or dead. After much careful thought, the woman responds that she does not know if the bird is dead or alive, but it exists in their hands. Morrison draws parallels between the bird and language and the old woman and the writer. The old woman passes the responsibility of preserving language to the children, and the youths respond. They passionately confess that adults hold keys to understanding the children's pasts, and they want to know everything. Pleased with their response, the old woman tells the children that even though they caught the bird, it was not in their hands.

VOCABULARY

The following words are defined in the glossary:

countenance	(890)	throttle	(890)	cataclysmic	(891)
mutant	(890)	languishing	(891)	sanctify	(891)

ANSWER KEYS

STUDY GUIDE

1. Nobel Prize for literature
2. She uses symbolism, foreshadowing, and flashbacks.
3. She compares the old woman to the writer, the bird to language.
4. It is the writer's responsibility to preserve, protect, and use language wisely.
5. The one who uses language
6. The youth indicate that their question was legitimate. Adults have a responsibility to use language to help them understand their own history.
7. Interpretations will vary.

BUILDING VOCABULARY

Students will identify various context clues. Definitions are given below.
1. teacher; wise person, usually of advanced age
2. concern with self; self-love
3. obstructs, frustrates, prevents
4. death, ruin
5. person who seizes power through unethical means

Study Guide

Toni Morrison (1931–)   NOBEL LECTURE IN LITERATURE   *(Page 888)*

Understanding the Writer and Her Background

1. What prestigious literary award did Morrison win in 1993?

_____

2. What three literary devices does Morrison use in her fiction?

_____

_____

_____

Understanding the Selection

3. What analogy does Morrison draw in her lecture about language and the writer?

_____

_____

_____

_____

4. What is Morrison's attitude about language?

_____

_____

_____

_____

5. Who is responsible for the fate of language?

_____

_____

continued ☞

NAME _____

CLASS_____ DATE _____

6. In the parable Morrison told, what is the youths' response to the old woman saying whether the bird lives or dies is their responsibility?

_____

_____

_____

_____

Writing and Responding to Literature

7. Morrison wrote, "We die. That may be the meaning of life. But we do language. That may be the measure of our lives." Write a paragraph explaining what you think this means. Use evidence from the lecture to support your comments.

_____

_____

_____

_____

_____

_____

_____

_____

_____

_____

_____

_____

_____

_____

_____

Building Vocabulary

Nobel Lecture in Literature   *Toni Morrison*   *(Page 888)*

———— IDENTIFYING CONTEXT CLUES ————

The words that surround a particular word in a sentence or paragraph are called the context of that word. In many cases, the context of a word can provide clues about that word's meaning.

> Soon after sundown, the *nocturnal* creatures of the desert begin to stir and venture out of their dens and nests.

In this example, the phrases "Soon after sundown" and "venture out of their dens and nests" indicate that "the nocturnal creatures of the desert" become active after dark. Consequently, these clues reveal that the word *nocturnal* means "active during the nighttime."

Write the word or words from the context that serve as clues to the meaning of the italicized word in each of the following passages. Then write the definition of the italicized word. *(25 points each)*

1. "Once upon a time there was an old woman. Blind but wise." Or was it an old man? A *guru*, perhaps. Or a griot soothing restless children.

   CONTEXT CLUE(S) _____

   MEANING _____

2. Like statist language, censored and censoring. Ruthless in its policing duties, it has no desire or purpose other than maintaining the free range of its own narcotic *narcissism*, its own exclusivity and dominance.

   CONTEXT CLUE(S) _____

   MEANING _____

3. . . . it is not without effect for it actively *thwarts* the intellect, stalls conscience, suppresses human potential.

   CONTEXT CLUE(S) _____

   MEANING _____

4. She is convinced that when language dies, out of carelessness, disuse, and absence of esteem, indifference or killed by fiat, not only she herself, but all users and makers are accountable for its *demise*.

   CONTEXT CLUE(S) _____

   MEANING _____

TIN LIZZIE   *John Dos Passos*   Text Page 894

OBJECTIVES

The aims of this lesson are for the student:
- To analyze Dos Passos' use of ironic tone to create an unflattering portrait of Henry Ford
- To define "impressionistic biography" and explain why "Tin Lizzie" fits into that category
- To stage a press conference
- To discuss what aspects of industrial society Charlie Chaplin's film *Modern Times* satirizes

INTRODUCING THE SELECTION

In *The New York Times* obituary article of September 29, 1970, a number of critical assessments of John Dos Passos and his work appeared, ranging from the positive to the negative. On the one hand Charles Poore, speaking of *U.S.A.*, said, "I think no modern novelist has got so much of it [the United States] into a book." Thomas Lask, also referring to this book, said, "Mr. Dos Passos may become known as the author of one book, but in its range and reach, in its willingness to meet head-on the possibilities of American life, it is large enough to be considered a life's work." On the other hand, Robie Macauley stated, "He sees things with the clarity and coolness of the camera's eye, which accounts for one of his faults. . . . His two-dimensional vision tends to create types." Perhaps the range of critical opinion Dos Passos has always elicited may be explained in part by the shift in his life and fiction from the political left to the political right. However, the author did not view this shift as contradictory because he always maintained that his allegiance was to the individual attempting to survive in a mechanistic world. For example, he said in 1939, "My sympathies lie with the private in the front line against the brass hat . . . with the laboratory worker against the stuffed shirt."

When introducing the Dos Passos selection, you should tell the students that it is included in the writer's master work, *U.S.A.* (1938). This experimental fiction is composed of three separate but interrelated novels entitled *The 42nd Parallel* (1930), *1919* (1932), and *The Big Money* (1936). In each of these, the author employs four distinct techniques: narratives involving the fictional characters; the Newsreel (collages of "newspaper quotations, political oratory, popular songs"); the Camera Eye ("impressionistic prose poems capturing poignant or decisive moments in the narrator's life"); and short biographical sketches of famous contemporary politicians (such as Eugene Debs), capitalists (such as Andrew Carnegie), inventors (such as Thomas Edison), performers (such as Isadora Duncan), and others. "Tin Lizzie" is the second biographical sketch in *The Big Money*.

SUMMARY

A vivid but slanted picture of Henry Ford as a clean-living American with revolutionary ideas about mechanical buggies and mass production but with only a superficial understanding of human nature or true genius emerges from this impressionistic biography. In a style that shifts abruptly like a Model T, Dos Passos subtly mocks Ford's inventiveness and his highly regarded business acumen. Fascinated by machinery, Ford was thrifty and never smoked, drank, or gambled. He left his father's farm when he was sixteen to work in a Detroit machine shop where he devoted his time to building a new gasoline engine. By 1900, when he was thirty-seven, he had a practicable car to promote. At forty, he started the Ford Motor Company and introduced the Model T, or "Tin Lizzie," in 1909. To Dos Passos' dismay and amusement this simple, uninspired man became the largest automobile manufacturer in the world, an industrial hero.

continued ☞

Analyzing the Use of Language

Before students begin their reading, ask students to discuss their opinions of corporate executives. Encourage students to consider what the executive's personality traits are likely to be, what the executive feels about the people who work for him, etc. Ask that students characterize each other's responses as positive, negative, or neutral. What words, phrases, or examples provide the clue? Tell students to consider how Dos Passos uses language to make his opinions of Henry Ford clear. Students might benefit from keeping a chart like the one below. After students have completed their reading, ask them to share their findings and to discuss reasons for their disagreements. Be prepared for a variety of responses, since student judgments are likely to vary widely. Do students consider this a positive, negative, or neutral portrait of Henry Ford?

Positive Comments	Neutral Comments	Negative Comments
	Ford left farm to get a job in a machine shop	

VOCABULARY   The words *sog(ging)* (page 896) and *inducement* (page 897) are defined in the glossary.

ANSWER KEYS

READING CHECK

A.
1. F
2. T
3. T
4. F
5. F

B. Summaries will vary.

STUDY GUIDE

1. *U.S.A.*, his complete work, consists of *The 42nd Parallel, 1919,* and *The Big Money.*
2. Possible answers include: 1) "But it had always been his custom to hire others to do the heavy work" (page 896); 2) ". . . maybe if the steady workers thought they were getting a cut (a very small cut) in the profits, it would give trained men an inducement to stick to their jobs . . ." (page 897).
3. Possible answers include: 1) he left his father's farm at age sixteen; 2) he met Edison in the late 1880s; 3) he produced the first Model T in 1909.
4. Students' examples will vary. They should note that Dos Passos' biography would have appeared more conventional, ordinary, and objective if he had not used the devices mentioned above.
5. Paragraphs will vary.

John Dos Passos   *Tin Lizzie*

(Page 895)

────────────────────── **READING CHECK** ──────────────────────

A. **True/False.** Write T for a true statement. Write F for a false statement.

_____   **1.** Henry Ford loved working on the farm.

_____   **2.** Ford used automobile races to promote his cars.

_____   **3.** Ford's Model T was known as the "Tin Lizzie."

_____   **4.** Of all automobile manufacturers, Ford paid the lowest wages.

_____   **5.** Ford's factories were among the last to adopt the assembly line.

B. Write a summary of "Tin Lizzie." As you write your summary, remember to

1. state ideas clearly and briefly,

2. state major points made by the author,

3. include all main ideas (but do not include ideas not in "Tin Lizzie"),

4. present the ideas in the order they were given,

5. keep your summary to one or two brief paragraphs.

_____

_____

_____

_____

_____

_____

_____

_____

_____

_____

_____

_____

Study Guide

John Dos Passos (1896–1970)

TIN LIZZIE   *(Pages 894–898)*

Understanding the Writer and His Background

1. John Dos Passos is best known for a trilogy of novels. Identify each of the novels in the trilogy, as well as the name under which the complete work was published.

_____

_____

_____

Understanding the Selection

2. Dos Passos' selection of detail and his tone suggest that he is mocking Ford's contributions to American life. Find two examples of sentences that seem to mock Ford.

_____

_____

_____

_____

_____

3. List three events in Dos Passos' account of Henry Ford's life that could be labeled objective by historical biographers.

_____

_____

_____

_____

_____

continued ☞

Understanding Literary Elements

4. Examine the punctuation, capitalization, and language used in "Tin Lizzie." Identify at least three examples of unconventional punctuation, unconventional capitalization, and slang words and phrases. Explain how the effect might have been different if Dos Passos had used conventional punctuation and capitalization and slang words and phrases.

_____

_____

_____

_____

_____

Writing and Responding to Literature

5. In "Tin Lizzie" John Dos Passos presents one impression of Henry Ford's character. In a paragraph or two, explain the impression that John Dos Passos presents. Discuss whether you think it is an appropriate impression; if you favor another view of Ford's character, explain what view that would be. For example, based on what you know about Henry Ford's life from other sources, should he be portrayed as a genius, a great leader, an American hero?

_____

_____

_____

_____

_____

_____

_____

_____

_____

_____

TEACHER'S NOTES

from DUST TRACKS ON A ROAD
Zora Neale Hurston

Text Page 899

OBJECTIVES

The aims of this lesson are for the student:
- To interpret idiomatic expressions and explain why they are effective in the excerpt from *Dust Tracks on a Road*
- To characterize the young Zora from information presented in the excerpt from *Dust Tracks on a Road*
- To write an essay discussing Hurston's reading tastes, citing evidence from the excerpt from *Dust Tracks on a Road*

INTRODUCING THE SELECTION

Zora Neale Hurston's outstanding contribution to American literature may well be her ability to capture in vivid prose the everyday experiences of life in the rural South. Her prose reflects an ability to capture the speech patterns of the people about whom she writes and an attention to detail so fresh that the reader is immediately immersed in the black life of the South.

Hurston's experience of small-town life in the South and her study of anthropology and speech patterns have given her the tools to speak accurately and eloquently of her heritage and to become a central figure in the Harlem Renaissance. Judith Wilson notes that what makes Hurston unique is her proud acknowledgment that black speech and mythology are just as valuable as white culture's "grammar and philosophy."

Hurston's novels all reflect this positive view of the black in America: *Their Eyes Were Watching God,* generally considered her greatest work, and *Seraph on the Suwannee* dramatize the lives of simple, loving black women while *Jonah's Gourd Vine* and *Moses: Man of the Mountain* both reflect the religious practices of blacks in the rural South.

Dust Tracks on a Road, from which the excerpt in the anthology is taken, attests to the author's positive view of blacks and their future.

SUMMARY

In this excerpt from her autobiography, Hurston describes a special association she had in grade school with two white women. She first sees the women from Minnesota when they unexpectedly visit her school in Florida one day. Apparently, whites from the North enjoyed visiting black schools around the turn of the century. The teacher asks Hurston's fifth-grade class to read aloud a Greco-Roman myth, one of the young Hurston's favorites. She excels in her reading, and the women are impressed. Afterwards, she meets the women and is invited to visit them the next day at their hotel. The women serve refreshments, talk to her, have her read to them, take her picture, and give her a present of one hundred new pennies. They send her books the next day, and after their return home send her clothes (which hold little interest for her) and more books (which open up many new worlds for her).

READING/CRITICAL THINKING STRATEGIES

Drawing Conclusions

Before students begin their reading, you might ask them to discuss any or all of the following: What did they like or dislike about elementary school? What gifts did they receive as children that seem particularly valuable to them now? Tell students to consider how Hurston would answer these questions. After students have completed their reading, ask them to share their responses and to discuss why Hurston chose to write about this incident.

continued ☞

VOCABULARY The following words are defined in the glossary:

caper	(900)	exalt (ed)	(901)	profound (ly)	(903)
squelch (er)	(900)	avarice	(902)	resolve (ed)	(903)
fluster (ed)	(900)				

ANSWER KEYS

STUDY GUIDE

1. Folk materials and anthropological research
2. Mrs. Johnstone and Miss Hurd apparently have come to the school to select a student they can "sponsor" by providing him or her with various books and materials.
3. She seems to be both confused and delighted by their visit and attention.
4. She enjoyed the story of Hercules but found stories about "this and that sweet and gentle little girl" to be "thin."
5. "Mrs. Calhoun always stood in the back, with a palmetto switch in her hand as a squelcher" (page 900). Definitions should suggest the meaning of "something that suppresses or silences completely." "It was not avarice that moved me" (page 902). Definitions should suggest the meaning of "desire for wealth."
6. Possible idioms: "Oh, I'm going to catch it now" (page 902); "I stuck to the pretty ones" (page 903); "The tricks and turns . . . left me cold." (page 903); ". . . amounted to a hill of beans" (page 903); ". . . kicked the bucket" (page 903); "They had no meat on their bones" (page 903). Explanations will vary.
7. Paragraphs and explanations will vary.

LANGUAGE SKILLS

A. 1. spatial order
   2. chronological order
   3. order of importance
   4. spatial order
   5. order of importance

B. 6. a. alarm clock
      b. breakfast
      c. school
      d. part-time job
      e. supper
      f. sleep
   7. a. sidewalk
      b. steps
      c. porch
      d. door
      e. attic window
      f. roof
   8. a. skeleton/shell
      b. claws/fingers
      c. antennae/ears
   9. a. mayor
      b. governor
      c. senator
      d. vice-president
      e. president

C. Answers may vary slightly; possible answers are provided.
   10. order of importance
   11. chronological order
   12. comparison/contrast
   13. spatial order
   14. order of importance
   15. spatial order

D. Students' paragraphs will vary.

BUILDING VOCABULARY

The italicized words are appropriate in the following sentences: 3, 5, 6, and 11. Students' revisions will vary.

Zora Neale Hurston (1891?–1960)

from **DUST TRACKS ON A ROAD** *(Pages 899–904)*

Understanding the Writer and Her Background

1. From what sources did Zora Neale Hurston obtain her ideas for *Mules and Men* (1935), her most popular book?

_____

_____

Understanding the Selection

2. Who are the two women who visit Zora's school, and why have they come?

_____

_____

_____

3. How does Zora react to their visit and to the attention they give her?

_____

_____

_____

4. Throughout the selection young Zora gives her opinion about certain books or stories. Describe her reactions to the story of Hercules as compared to the stories about "this and that sweet . . . little girl."

_____

_____

_____

_____

continued ☞

Understanding Vocabulary

5. Find the sentences in the selection in which the following words appear. Write the sentence and then write a brief definition of the word as it is used in the sentence. Check your definition in the glossary.

squelch(er) (page 900) _____

_____

_____

_____

avarice (page 902) _____

_____

_____

_____

Understanding Literary Elements

6. Idioms are expressions that, while they may not make sense literally, have a special meaning to the speakers of the language. For example, when someone says, "Don't lose your head," people who speak American English know that it does not mean that the person might not be able to find his or her head. Zora Neale Hurston's use of idiomatic speech patterns brings the sounds of oral speech to her writing. Identify at least three idioms used by Hurston in this selection and explain what they mean.

_____

_____

_____

_____

_____

_____

_____

_____

_____

Writing and Responding to Literature

7. Hurston's use of idiomatic speech patterns creates an informal, personal tone. Rewrite the third paragraph in the selection, using standard, non-idiomatic language. Then, write one or two sentences explaining how the change in language affects the tone of the paragraph.

Paragraph _____

_____

_____

_____

_____

_____

_____

_____

_____

_____

_____

_____

Explanation _____

_____

_____

_____

_____

from **Dust Tracks on a Road**   *Zora Neale Hurston*   *(Page 900)*

──────── ORDER OF IDEAS ────────

Writers convey their meaning clearly by presenting their ideas in a logical order. As you read the following excerpt, note how the details are arranged.

> "Yes, Jupiter had seen her (Persephone). He had seen the maiden picking flowers in the field. He had seen the chariot of the dark monarch pause by the maiden's side. He had seen him when he seized Persephone. He had seen the black horses leap down Mount Aetna's fiery throat. Persephone was now in Pluto's dark realm and he had made her his wife." *(Page 901)*

The details in this paragraph are arranged in chronological, or time, order, the order in which the events occurred. Chronological order is one of four basic ways to arrange ideas.

Chronological order: sequence of events or steps
Spatial order: placement in space (left to right, top to bottom, etc.)
Order by comparison/contrast: similar features, different features
Order of importance: relative importance (least to most, worst to best, etc.)

ACTIVITY A

In the blank before the numbers, write the kind of order used to arrange details in the excerpts.

_____ 1. They had shiny hair, mostly brownish. One had a looping gold chain around her neck. The other one was dressed all over in black and white. . . . But the thing that held my eyes were their fingers. *(Page 900)*

_____ 2. The class was dismissed and the visitors smiled us away and went into a low-voiced conversation with Mr. Calhoun for a few minutes. *(Page 901)*

_____ 3. They asked me if I loved school, and I lied that I did. There was *some* truth in it, because I liked geography and reading, and I liked to play at recess time. Whoever it was invented writing and arithmetic got no thanks from me. *(Page 902)*

continued ☞

_____   **4.** My sandy hair sported a red ribbon to match my red and white checked gingham dress, starched until it could stand alone. Mama saw to it that my shoes were on the right feet. . . .   *(Page 902)*

_____   **5.** In that box were *Gulliver's Travels, Grimm's Fairy Tales, Dick Whittington, Greek and Roman Myths,* and best of all, *Norse Tales.*   *(Page 903)*

ACTIVITY B

Arrange the listed items according to the type of order specified.

6. *Chronological:* alarm clock, sleep, school, supper, breakfast, part-time job

   a. _____   **c.** _____   **e.** _____

   b. _____   **d.** _____   **f.** _____

7. *Spatial:* attic window, sidewalk, porch, door, steps, roof

   a. _____   **c.** _____   **e.** _____

   b. _____   **d.** _____   **f.** _____

8. *Comparison or Contrast (in pairs):* skeleton, claws, shell, antennae, fingers, ears

   a. _____/_____   **b.** _____/_____   **c.** _____/_____

9. *Importance (least to most):* President, governor, senator, mayor, Vice-President

   a. _____   **c.** _____   **e.** _____

   b. _____   **d.** _____

ACTIVITY C

In each blank, write the kind of order you think would be appropriate for a paragraph on the topic.

10. foods you dislike _____

11. how you spent last Saturday _____

12. two pets you have owned _____

13. the inside of your locker _____

14. reasons to go (or not to go) to college _____

15. a park in your neighborhood _____

continued ☞

ACTIVITY D

Write a paragraph on one of the topics in ACTIVITY C, using the kind of order you selected for that topic.

_____

_____

_____

_____

_____

_____

_____

_____

_____

_____

_____

_____

_____

Building Vocabulary

Zora Neale Hurston from *Dust Tracks on a Road* (Page 900)

───────────────── **ANALYZING WORDS IN CONTEXT** ─────────────────

ACTIVITY

In the following sentences, some of the italicized words, which are from *Dust Tracks on a Road*, are used inappropriately in the context of the sentence. If an italicized word is inappropriate, cross through the part of the sentence that creates an inappropriate context. Then, rewrite the sentence so that the word is used correctly. If the word is used appropriately, leave the sentence alone and identify it as correct.

1. Thanks to that little *caper* we pulled in class, we have been named to the school honor roll.

_____

_____

2. My employer's kind comments praising my job performance were such a *squelcher* that I decided to quit.

_____

_____

3. As I walked across the stage to receive my diploma, I was so *flustered* by the thought of everyone looking at me that I tripped and fell.

_____

_____

4. In our society, television newscasters enjoy such *exalted* status that most viewers don't even know their names.

_____

_____

5. In a historic move, King Henry VIII declared that all holdings of the Catholic church within his *realm* belonged to him.

_____

_____

continued ☞

6. Although the original plan was to share the treasure, each of the pirates, motivated by *avarice*, attempted to escape with the entire horde of gold.

_____

_____

7. Squirming restlessly from boredom, the audience appeared *profoundly* moved by the speaker's words.

_____

_____

8. Hearing suppressed *snickers* throughout the room, the teacher knew immediately that the students were taking the lesson seriously.

_____

_____

9. The young children had such a reputation for their *angelic* behavior that it was becoming impossible to find a baby-sitter for them.

_____

_____

10. Correctly worn, a Scottish *tam* ends just above the knee.

_____

_____

11. The bitterly cold air *tingled* the bare arms of the inappropriately dressed tourists.

_____

_____

CIRCUS AT DAWN   *Thomas Wolfe*   Text Page 905

OBJECTIVES   The aims of this lesson are for the student:
- To explain elements of characterization and discuss the effectiveness of setting in "Circus at Dawn"
- To find descriptive phrases that are appealing to the senses
- To form an opinion on the adult perspective of childhood experiences and support the opinion with examples
- To find examples of and explain the effect of stylistic devices in "Circus at Dawn"

INTRODUCING THE SELECTION   "We are the sum of all the moments of our lives—all that is ours is in them; we cannot escape or conceal it." These words of Thomas Wolfe, written in the introduction to his long novel *Look Homeward, Angel,* can give your class a clue to his method of writing.

As a man, Wolfe wanted to experience everything. As a writer, he wanted to describe that experience fully. Quite often he focused more attention on the sordid and unpleasant parts of his experience. He wrote so voluminously that it was usually a monumental task for an editor to help him compress his manuscripts to publishable size. According to Maxwell Perkins, the most important of Wolfe's editors, the type-script for *Of Time and the River* made a pile two feet high, and it took a year of cutting and arguing before author and editor could arrive at a final version, in which some scenes were reduced by two-thirds. Said Perkins, "There never was any cutting that Tom did not agree to. He knew that cutting was necessary. His whole impulse was to utter what he felt and he had no time to revise and compress."

Despite the editorial paring, all of Wolfe's books were big. He once told Sherwood Anderson that, although there might be better ways to write a novel that to "pour it out, boil it out, flood it out," he had to work in his own way. Sometimes when cuts and revisions were suggested, his revised chapters would turn out to be longer than the original ones.

You may tell students that Wolfe kept notebooks full of facts that he accumulated for possible use in his novel *Look Homeward, Angel.* Nothing was unimportant to him. He even made notes on rooms he had slept in—the way chairs creaked and towels hung, the designs of the wallpaper, and the water stains on the ceilings.

As you assign this selection, ask the students to notice the descriptions of sights, sounds, and smells which Wolfe uses to recount the rapture of the small boy watching the arrival of the circus. How is this description accomplished? Does Wolfe use metaphor to a great extent? How sharp and clear are these descriptions?

SUMMARY   With characteristic exuberance and interest in sensory details, Wolfe describes what it was like for him as a child when a big circus came to town. He would hurriedly finish his paper route and wake his brother. Together they would take a streetcar or get a ride to the train depot to see the circus people. The boys inhaled the mixture of train smells and circus smells and listened to the sounds of the circus people as they began to set things up. The two boys enjoyed watching the workers' "orderly confusion," the elephants helping to put up the tents, and the circus crew eating their enormous breakfasts. Observing all the circus activity would make the two boys hungry, and they would have to stop in town and eat before going home to a big breakfast.

continued ☞

READING/CRITICAL THINKING STRATEGIES

Finding Significant Details

Before students begin their reading, ask them to think about the cafeteria at lunch hour. Encourage student to freewrite for one or two minutes in response to each of the following questions: What do you see in the cafeteria? What do you smell? What do you hear? What do you taste? Ask students to share some of their responses. Remind students that it is details like these that make for good descriptive writing. Tell students to make a chart in which they list the sensory details they find particularly effective. You may want to use the chart below as an example. After students have completed their reading, ask them to compare their findings.

Sight	Smell	Sound	Taste	Touch
		low, excited voices		cool

ANSWER KEYS

READING CHECK

A. 1. F
   2. F
   3. T
   4. T
   5. T

B. Early morning when the circus is unloading, on the circus grounds when the tents are being put up, in the circus tent while the performers are eating breakfast

STUDY GUIDE

1. He helped Wolfe trim and shape great piles of manuscript into Wolfe's first novel, *Look Homeward, Angel.*

2. Height and ambition
3. He describes his father's "shabby little marble shop," the train depot, and the circus grounds in the autumn morning.
4. Possible responses include: 1) "fine-looking people, strong and handsome"; 2) "speaking and moving with an almost stern dignity and decorum"; 3) "a handsome and magnificent young woman with blond hair and the figure of an Amazon"; 4) "a powerfully built, thickset man of middle age, who had a stern, lined, responsible-looking face and a bald head"; 5) ". . . in a perilous and beautiful exhibition of human balance and precision."
5. Explanations will vary.

Thomas Wolfe   *Circus at Dawn*   *(Page 906)*

──────── READING CHECK ────────

A. True/False. Write T for a true statement. Write F for a false statement.

_____ **1.** The circus came to town in July of every year.

_____ **2.** The boy went to the circus grounds with his younger brother and sister.

_____ **3.** The narrator was impressed by the smells of the circus.

_____ **4.** Some of the circus performers lived in sumptuous-looking railroad cars.

_____ **5.** One of the trapeze artists was a thickset man of middle age.

B. Identify three scenes or events described by Wolfe in "Circus at Dawn" in the order in which he experiences them.

_____

_____

_____

_____

_____

_____

_____

_____

_____

_____

_____

_____

_____

_____

Study Guide

Thomas Wolfe (1900–1938)

CIRCUS AT DAWN *(Pages 906–909)*

Understanding the Writer and His Background

1. How was Maxwell Perkins instrumental in helping Thomas Wolfe become a successful writer?

_____

_____

_____

2. Identify a physical trait and a personality trait that Thomas Wolfe had in common with

Eugene Gant, the main character of his first two novels. _____

_____

Understanding the Selection

3. Wolfe uses chronological order to unify his memories about a visit to the circus. What are the three main settings he describes?

_____

_____

_____

4. In Wolfe's view as a child, the circus performers are superior people. List five descriptive details Wolfe uses that reveal his view of the performers.

_____

_____

_____

_____

_____

_____

continued ☞

Writing and Responding to Literature

5. Wolfe's writing is characterized by the use of many details, many adjectives and adverbs, and long, involved sentences. Compare the following paraphrase with the original paragraph on page 908. Write a few sentences explaining which version you feel is more effective and why.

> Meanwhile, the food tent—a huge top without sides—had been put up. Now we could see the performers seated at tables underneath the tent, as they ate breakfast. The savor of the food they ate was mixed with our excitement, the smells of the animals, the glory of the morning, and the coming of the circus. As a result, it seemed to be the most succulent we had ever known or eaten.

_____

_____

_____

_____

_____

_____

_____

_____

_____

_____

_____

_____

TEACHER'S NOTES

from BLACK BOY *Richard Wright*

Text Page 910

OBJECTIVES

The aims of this lesson are for the student:
- To identify details from and interpret meaning in an excerpt from *Black Boy*
- To explain and support Wright's description of himself in an excerpt from *Black Boy*
- To write an essay about a major influence in the student's life and explain how it contributed to the student's understanding of character

INTRODUCING THE SELECTION

In addition to the biographical material supplied by the text, it is important to note that Richard Wright, during the course of his life, sought answers to social and racial problems found in the United States by associating himself with various ideologies, among them naturalism, existentialism, and African nationalism. As stated in the preface to a selection by Wright in *Black American Literature: 1760–Present* (1971), "Whatever system he advocated for the restoration of social justice, one idea pervades his writing: that the root of evil does lie in the society, never in the man."

Aside from his novel, *Native Son* (1940), Richard Wright's autobiography, *Black Boy* (1945), is probably the most acclaimed piece of writing he ever published. The book treats Wright's painful childhood and adolescence up to the time he abandoned the South in search of a better life in the North. Its concluding paragraph reads:

> With ever watchful eyes and bearing scars, visible and invisible, I headed North, full of a hazy notion that life could be lived with dignity, that the personalities of others should not be violated, that men should be able to confront other men without fear or shame, and that if men were lucky in their living on earth they might win some redeeming meaning for their having struggled and suffered here beneath the stars.

This is the context of the present selection, which has been taken from the opening chapter of *American Hunger* (posthumously published in 1977), the author's auto-biographical sequel to *Black Boy*.

When assigning the selection, ask the students to note the discrepancy between Wright's hope at the end of *Black Boy* "that life could be lived with dignity" in the North and the actual circumstances of his existence once he reaches Chicago.

SUMMARY

This excerpt from *Black Boy*, the second part of Richard Wright's autobiography, relates Wright's attempts to find employment and to perfect his writing skills after his arrival in Chicago in 1927. Wright describes himself as a loner, an emotionally and psychologically self-sufficient person who had no friends. He lived to write, and he created narratives about people in his environment, the urban black ghetto, whenever he was not working. He worked first at a cafe and then at the post office as a temporary clerk. Unable to gain enough weight to meet the requirements for a full-time clerk's position, Wright returned to work at the cafe. He was "hungry for insight" into life, and he wrote constantly. By age twenty, Wright says, the mold of his life was set.

READING/CRITICAL THINKING STRATEGIES

Finding Cause-and-Effect Relationships

Before students begin their reading, ask them to consider how a life change (such as a change of schools, the birth of a sibling, the loss of a friend, or the acquisition of a pet) has affected them. Did it set a series of events and reactions into motion? Encourage students to consider hypothetical situations: a woman who has been a housewife and mother for ten years goes back to work at a high salary. What are likely

continued ☞

to be the effects? How might one effect cause another? Tell students that as they read they should look for cause-and-effect relationships in Wright's work. Students might benefit from keeping a chart like the one below. After students have completed their reading, ask them to compare their findings. Ask students to discuss the last sentence of the essay. What do they think causes Wright to make this statement? What do they think it means?

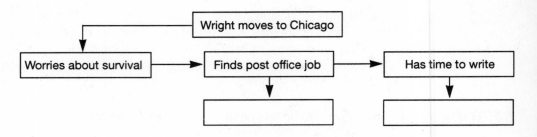

VOCABULARY

The following words are defined in the glossary:

reprisal	(912)	complement	(913)	integral	(913)
disconsolate (ly)	(913)	usurp (ed)	(913)	libation (s)	(913)
decadence	(913)				

ANSWER KEYS

READING CHECK

A.
1. T
2. F
3. F
4. T
5. T

B. Answers will vary. Major events include: he arrives in Chicago and finds work; he writes in his spare time and hopes for a permanent position as a postal clerk; because of earlier malnutrition, he cannot gain enough weight to pass the physical exam; reading and writing consume most of his time other than work; he finally passes the postal exam; he states that his life patterns were set by the age of twenty.

STUDY GUIDE

1. It brought unprecedented attention to black literature and to black writers.
2. *Black Boy*
3. He obtained a job, which enabled him to eat, and he read and wrote voraciously.

4. He only wanted a job; diversion and satisfying human relationships were unknown to him.
5. Possible answers include: 1) His description of his behavior at "house-rent" parties, and 2) his description of his "terse, cynical mode of speech" (page 912).
6. Definitions should suggest the meaning "retaliation."

   Definitions should suggest the meaning "essential."
7. Sentences will vary.

BUILDING VOCABULARY

A.
1. a, c, g
2. e
3. f
4. f
5. b, h
6. h
7. g
8. a
9. d, f
10. h
11. b
12. c
13. g
14. d

B. Answers will vary.

NAME _____

CLASS _____ DATE _____ SCORE _____

Richard Wright   from *Black Boy*   *(Page 911)*

—————————————— READING CHECK ——————————————

A. True/False. Write T for a true statement. Write F for a false statement.

_____ **1.** Wright depicts himself as he was at the age of twenty.

_____ **2.** He was a friendly, sociable person.

_____ **3.** He could not pass the post office test because he was overweight.

_____ **4.** Wright struggled to improve his writing style by turning out series of disconnected sentences.

_____ **5.** Wright was caught up in an inner world of his own thoughts and feelings.

B. List the major events in this excerpt from *Black Boy* in the order in which they occurred.

_____

_____

_____

_____

_____

_____

_____

_____

_____

_____

_____

_____

_____

_____

_____

Study
Guide

Richard Wright (1908–1960)

from **BLACK BOY** *(Pages 910–914)*

Understanding the Writer and His Background

1. What important contribution to American literature did Wright make in his first novel, *Native Son?*

_____

_____

2. Name Wright's autobiographical novel about his experiences growing up in the South.

_____

Understanding the Selection

3. How was life in Chicago better for Wright than life had been in the South?

_____

_____

4. In the second paragraph, Wright says that his expectations were modest. What were his expectations and desires?

_____

_____

5. In this autobiographical account, Wright describes himself as being of a "fiercely indrawn nature." Identify two descriptions of his actions that support this assessment.

_____

_____

_____

_____

continued ☞

Understanding Vocabulary

6. The following words are from the selection by Richard Wright. Determine each word's meaning by using the context; then in your own words, write the meaning of each word.

reprisal (page 912)

_____

_____

integral (page 913)

_____

_____

Writing and Responding to Literature

7. When Wright practiced writing, his "purpose was to capture a physical state or movement that carried a strong subjective impression. . . ." Rewrite the three sentences he uses as examples of this technique (page 912, second column) and change them to more objective observations.

(1) _____

_____

_____

_____

(2) _____

_____

_____

_____

(3) _____

_____

_____

_____

NAME _____

CLASS _____ DATE _____ SCORE _____

Richard Wright   from *Black Boy*   (Page 911)

——————————— **PRACTICING DICTIONARY SKILLS** ———————————

ACTIVITY A

For this activity, use a dictionary that shows etymologies, parts of speech, and synonyms and antonyms, as well as multiple meanings. The numbered statements below describe one or more of the following vocabulary words from *Black Boy*. Use your dictionary to determine which word or words are described by each statement. Then place the letter or letters of the appropriate vocabulary word or words in the blank before each statement.

a. reprisal	**c.** decadence	**e.** usurped	**g.** libation
b. disconsolate	**d.** complement	**f.** integral	**h.** translucent

_____ **1.** Used only as a noun

_____ **2.** The past tense of a transitive or intransitive verb

_____ **3.** Can be an adjective or a noun

_____ **4.** Antonym of *nonessential*

_____ **5.** Used only as an adjective

_____ **6.** From a Latin word meaning "to shine through"

_____ **7.** One meaning involves a ceremony

_____ **8.** From an Italian word meaning "to take back"

_____ **9.** The meaning depends on the pronunciation

_____ **10.** A synonym of *clear*

_____ **11.** A synonym of *cheerless*

_____ **12.** From a French word meaning "a falling away"

_____ **13.** From a Latin word meaning "to taste"

_____ **14.** Has specialized meanings in grammar, math, and music

continued ☞

ACTIVITY B

Write your responses to the following questions on the blanks provided.

15. How might a *disconsolate* person sit or stand?

_____

_____

_____

16. In what sense is the maxim "An eye for an eye and a tooth for a tooth" a guideline for *reprisal*?

_____

_____

_____

17. Do you feel that physical education is an *integral* part of the school curriculum? Why?

_____

_____

_____

TEACHER'S NOTES

from THE WAY TO RAINY MOUNTAIN

N. Scott Momaday

OBJECTIVES

The aims of this lesson are for the student:
- To identify details from and interpret meaning in an excerpt from *The Way to Rainy Mountain*
- To explain how the Kiowas' lives were transformed
- To interpret Momaday's characterization of his mother
- To write an essay describing a special place and indicating influence through selection of details

INTRODUCING THE SELECTION

Whereas Wright confines himself to contemporary personal situations, Momaday travels backward through time to recreate a Native American past from which he has descended. When you assign the Momaday selection in the context of the previous three, you might ask the students to be aware of the differences between an autobiography that focuses on the present life of the author and an autobiography that uses the present life to invoke the past life of his or her group. What do these two kinds of autobiography suggest about the quest for personal and group identity?

SUMMARY

In *The Way to Rainy Mountain,* Momaday examines the history and culture of his people, the Kiowas in Oklahoma. This excerpt begins with a description of their lonely, harsh land. He returns one July to visit the grave of his grandmother, Aho, and reflects on her life and the Kiowas' past. Momaday describes the lands far away from Rainy Mountain about which his grandmother told stories—Yellowstone, the Rockies, and the Black Hills. In 1887, when she was about seven, his grandmother witnessed the end of the Kiowas' religious rituals; she saw the last Sun Dance. Looking back on the old woman's life, Momaday recalls his grandmother's routines, her house and its visitors, prayer meetings, and night feasts.

READING/CRITICAL THINKING STRATEGIES

Making Inferences

As a prereading strategy, ask students to discuss what they think is important about their cultural heritages. Give students who wish to do so the opportunity to discuss their ethnic backgrounds. Tell students to consider what Momaday finds valuable about his Kiowa heritage. Which values does Momaday state directly? Which have to be inferred? Students might benefit from keeping a chart like the one below. After students have finished their reading, ask them to share their findings and to discuss their reactions to Momaday's work.

	Inferred	Evidence
Values	Respect for elders	Decision to go to grave

	Stated	Direct Quotation
	Nomadic spirit	"ancient nomadic spirit was suddenly free of the ground"

continued 🖙

VOCABULARY

The following words are defined in the glossary:

preeminent (ly)	(916)	wean	(917)	impale	(919)
pillage	(916)	engender	(917)	enmity (–ies)	(920)
nomadic	(916)	tenuous	(917)	nocturnal	(920)
solstice (s)	(917)	consummate	(919)	purl (ed)	(920)

VOCABULARY ACTIVITY

Present to your class the following list of vocabulary words from the excerpt from *The Way to Rainy Mountain* in the textbook and the ten sentences that begin after the list. Have students identify the word from the list that fits in the blank of each sentence. Then, have students define each word as it is used in the sentence.

You can present the list and the sentences by writing them on the chalkboard or on a transparency and having students give answers orally or write them on their own paper. Or, you can distribute copies of the list and the sentences and have students write their answers on the copies. If you decide to use copies, be sure to leave sufficient space between sentences for students to write their answers.

pillage	nocturnal
nomads	enmities
solstices	impale
wean	tenuous
engender	purled
consummate	lees
preeminently	deicide
stonecrop	

1. In that rugged, windswept terrain, plants grow only on the _____ of the rocky outcroppings.

2. Most people prefer a(n) _____ sleeping schedule.

3. Many _____ on the Great Plains followed the yearly migrations of the buffalo herds.

4. Would you _____ two or three of those marshmallows on the end of this stick so that I can roast them in the fire?

5. Although the race was close, our candidate held a(n) _____ lead throughout the night.

6. That sort of rude, unkind behavior toward others is likely to _____ resentment and hard feelings in them.

7. The _____ of their vanquished enemies' towns and cities provided the raiders with the supplies they needed.

8. Although my mother has many artistic skills, she is _____ a painter and prefers to work in oils.

9. Are the summer and winter _____ exactly six months apart?

10. A team of negotiators worked long hours for several weeks, trying to hammer out a settlement despite the _____ that the warring factions felt toward one another.

Answers:

1. lees	6. engender
2. nocturnal	7. pillage
3. nomadic	8. preeminently
4. impale	9. solstices
5. tenuous	10. enmities

continued ☞

ANSWER KEYS

READING CHECK

from The Way to Rainy
Mountain   Text Page 916

A. 1. T   4. F
    2. T   5. T
    3. F

B. Answers will vary. Students should mention
   that Momaday visits his grandmother's grave
   and reflects on her life and the history of the
   Kiowa Indians. He chronicles the journey of
   the Kiowas from northern America to the
   Plains and their eventual defeat by the white
   men. He discusses the myths and religious
   beliefs he learned from his grandmother.

STUDY GUIDE

from The Way to Rainy
Mountain   Text Page 916

1. A young Native American's attempt to recon-
   cile the values of an old way of life with those
   of the modern world
2. Nonfiction: *The Way to Rainy Mountain, The
   Names;* poetry: *Angle of Geese and Other Poems*
   and *The Gourd Dancer*
3. He returns to Rainy Mountain to visit his
   grandmother's grave.
4. Momaday says they were no longer "slaves to
   the simple necessity of survival," that they were
   a "lordly and dangerous society of fighters and
   thieves, hunters and priests of the sun."
5. Tai-me was the sacred Sun Dance doll. In 1890
   the Kiowas came together to offer their ancient
   sacrifice to Tai-me, but before they could begin
   their dance, they were dispersed by soldiers
   from Fort Sill.
6. Answers will vary.
7. Summaries will vary but should include the following points: three centuries ago the Kiowas
   came down from Montana; in the late 1600s
   they migrated to the south and east, where
   they befriended the Crows and acquired horses

and Tai-me, the sacred Sun Dance doll; in
1887 the last Kiowa Sun Dance was held; on
July 20, 1890, the Kiowas were dispersed by soldiers from Fort Sill.

BUILDING VOCABULARY A

from The Way to Rainy
Mountain   Text Page 916

A. Answers will vary. The following are suggested
   answers.
   1. adjective; caused by tornadoes
   2. noun; state of being allies
   3. noun; state of being divine, or sacred
   4. adjective; given to being tentative, or not
      substantial
   5. noun; state of being wary, or cautious
   6. noun; state of being enemies
   7. adjective; pertaining to night
   8. adjective; pertaining to ancestors

B. Answers will vary.

BUILDING VOCABULARY B

from The Way to Rainy
Mountain   Text Page 916

1. lees   6. engender
2. nocturnal   7. pillage
3. nomadic   8. preeminently
4. impale   9. solstices
5. tenuous   10. enmities

SELECTION TEST

John Dos Passos, Zora Neale Hurston,
Thomas Wolfe, Richard Wright, N. Scott
Momaday

1. b   4. a
2. c   5. d
3. d

NAME _____

CLASS _____ DATE _____ SCORE _____

N. Scott Momaday   from *The Way to Rainy Mountain*   *(Page 916)*

———————————— **READING CHECK** ————————————

A. True/False. Write T for a true statement. Write F for a false statement.

_____ 1. Momaday returned to Rainy Mountain to visit his grandmother's grave.

_____ 2. The grandmother was a member of the Kiowas.

_____ 3. The Kiowas were driven into the Grand Canyon by the U.S. Cavalry.

_____ 4. Tai-me is the Kiowas' rain dance doll.

_____ 5. The Kiowas worship the sun.

B. Write a summary of this excerpt from *The Way to Rainy Mountain*. As you write your summary, remember to

1. state ideas clearly and briefly,

2. state the major point Momaday makes in this excerpt,

3. include all main ideas (but do not include ideas not in the excerpt),

4. present the major ideas in the order in which they are given,

5. keep your summary to one or two brief paragraphs.

_____

_____

_____

_____

_____

_____

_____

_____

_____

_____

_____

Study Guide

N. Scott Momaday (1934–   )

from **THE WAY TO RAINY MOUNTAIN**   *(Pages 915–921)*

Understanding the Writer and His Background

1. What was the subject of Momaday's first book, *House Made of Dawn* (1968)? _____

_____

_____

2. In addition to his novel, *House Made of Dawn*, what other works has Momaday published? Identify the name and the form (novel, poetry, nonfiction) of each work.

_____

_____

_____

Understanding the Selection

3. What event triggers Momaday's reflections about the history of the Kiowa Indians?

_____

_____

4. How did the Kiowas change as they moved from the mountains to the plains?

_____

_____

_____

_____

5. What was the Kiowas' symbol of worship? What brought an end to their annual rite of

worship? _____

_____

_____

continued ☞

Understanding Vocabulary

6. Explain how each of the words listed below is related to the history and characteristics of the Kiowas. Refer to the glossary if necessary.

pillage _____

_____

_____

nomadic _____

_____

_____

solstice(s) _____

_____

_____

nocturnal _____

_____

Writing and Responding to Literature

7. In this selection, Momaday tells the history of the Kiowa Indians. In your own words, write a brief summary of that history.

_____

_____

_____

_____

_____

_____

_____

_____

_____

N. Scott Momaday   from *The Way to Rainy Mountain*   *(Page 916)*

———————— **IDENTIFYING WORD PARTS / PRACTICING DICTIONARY SKILLS** ————————

A **suffix** is a word part that is added to the end of a word or a word root to give that word or root a new meaning.

EXAMPLE	**Word/Root**	**Suffix**	**Combined**
	employ	-ee	employee
	aristo	-crat	aristocrat

The **root** of a word is its core part. Many English words have roots originally derived from Greek or Latin. The word *pompous,* for example, comes from the Latin *pompa,* meaning "display" or "procession." The word *phototropic* is a compound of two Greek roots: *photos* ("light") and *tropos* ("responding to a stimulus"); consequently, a plant that is phototropic is one that responds to light.

ACTIVITY A

Below is a list of suffixes and their meanings. In each of the following sentences from *The Way to Rainy Mountain*, the italicized word is formed with one of these suffixes. Using a dictionary, identify the suffix and the word or root to which the suffix has been added. Then use the meaning of both the suffix and the word root to which the suffix is added, as well as the context of the sentence, to determine the meaning of the word as it is used in the sentence. Write each word's part of speech and definition on the blanks provided.

Suffix	**Meaning**
-al	doer, pertaining to
-ance, -ancy	act, condition, fact
-ic	dealing with, caused by, person or thing
-ity	state, quality, condition
-ness	quality, state
-ous	marked by, given to
-tion	action, condition

1. "Winter brings blizzards, hot *tornadic* winds arise in the spring, and in summer the prairie is an anvil's edge."

_____

_____

_____

continued ☞

2. "In *alliance* with the Comanches, they had ruled the whole of the southern Plains."

_____

_____

_____

3. "They acquired Tai-me, the sacred Sun Dance doll, from that moment the object and symbol of their worship and so shared in the *divinity* of the sun."

_____

_____

_____

4. "However *tenuous* their well-being, however much they had suffered and would suffer again, they had found a way out of the wilderness."

_____

_____

_____

5. "There was a *wariness* in her, and an ancient awe."

_____

_____

_____

6. "Some of them painted their faces and carried the scars of old and cherished *enmities*."

_____

_____

_____

7. "There were frequent prayer meetings and great *nocturnal* feasts."

_____

_____

_____

continued ☞

8. "Here and there on the dark stones were *ancestral* names."

_____

_____

_____

ACTIVITY B

In *The Way to Rainy Mountain,* the word *tornadic* is used to describe the spring winds, and the word *nomadic* is used to describe the spirit of the Kiowas. What words with the suffix *-ic* might be used to describe young people of your generation? Write those words below.

_____

_____

_____

_____

_____

_____

_____

N. Scott Momaday   from *The Way to Rainy Mountain*   *(Page 916)*

―――――――――― **USING WORDS IN CONTEXT** ――――――――――

From the following list of vocabulary words, choose the word that best completes the meaning in each sentence below.

pillage	wean	preeminently	enmities	purled
nomadic	engender	stonecrop	impale	lees
solstices	consumate	nocturnal	tenuous	deicide

1. In that rugged, windswept terrain, plants grow only on the _____ of the rocky outcroppings.

2. Most people prefer a(n) _____ sleeping schedule.

3. Many _____ tribes on the Great Plains followed the yearly migrations of the buffalo herds.

4. Would you _____ two or three of those marshmallows on the end of this stick so that I can roast them in the fire?

5. Although the race was close, our candidate held a(n) _____ lead throughout the night.

6. That sort of rude, unkind behavior toward others is likely to _____ resentment and hard feelings in them.

7. The _____ of their vanquished enemies' towns and cities provided the raiders with the supplies they needed.

8. Although my mother has many artistic skills, she is _____ a painter and prefers to work in oils.

9. Are the summer and winter _____ exactly six months apart?

10. A team of negotiators worked long hours, trying to hammer out a settlement despite

    the _____ that the warring factions felt toward one another.

John Dos Passos, Zora Neale Hurston, Thomas Wolfe, Richard Wright, N. Scott Momaday

AN OPEN-BOOK TEST

(Pages 894–921)

Directions: Write the letter of the *best* answer to each question. *(20 points each)*

1. Which of the following most accurately sums up Dos Passos' views about Henry Ford?
   a. The greatest American of all time
   b. One of our most influential innovators
   c. One of our foremost humanitarians
   d. A brilliant inventor but a second-rate salesperson

   1. _____

2. Zora Neale Hurston relates in *Dust Tracks on a Road* that when visitors arrive at her school, she and her classmates read aloud the
   a. story of Red Riding Hood
   b. adventures of Mowgli
   c. myth of the origin of the seasons
   d. myth of Thor and Odin

   2. _____

3. Unusual features of Thomas Wolfe's prose, as demonstrated in "Circus at Dawn," include all of the following *except*
   a. many vivid details
   b. long involved sentences
   c. generous use of adjectives and adverbs
   d. thoughtful, impersonal character analyses

   3. _____

4. In the excerpt from *Black Boy,* Richard Wright suggests that the danger of his late adolescence was
   a. getting lost in his fantasy life
   b. losing courage with regard to his writing
   c. giving in to the poverty in his life
   d. losing touch with his friends and relatives

   4. _____

5. N. Scott Momaday, in the excerpt from *The Way to Rainy Mountain,* draws a parallel between
   a. the Kiowa warriors and the United States Cavalry
   b. his own boyhood and the origins of the Kiowas
   c. the legends of the Devil's Tower and Rainy Mountain
   d. the death of his grandmother and the death of the Kiowas

   5. _____

TEACHER'S NOTES

MOTHER TONGUE   *Amy Tan*   Text Page 922

OBJECTIVES

The aims of this lesson are for the student:
- To understand Tan's attitude toward language
- To explain the effect of Tan's ending the essay with a phrase of "broken" English
- To recognize how Tan defines her writing style
- To consider audience when preparing notes for a problem-solution essay

INTRODUCING THE SELECTION

Amy Tan, writer of fiction, non-fiction, and children's literature, became critically and publicly acclaimed with the publication of *The Joy Luck Club*. She was instantly established as a gifted storyteller. In addition to *The Joy Luck Club* (1989), Tan has published two other books. *The Kitchen God's Wife* (1991) and *The Moon Lady* (1992), a children's book, mark the start of a rich tradition of tales from a great writer.

SUMMARY

While delivering a speech in formal English to a large audience, Tan realizes that she has used a variety of language forms. To understand the forms of English she uses, Tan tapes her mother telling a Chinese story in English. Some of Tan's friends have difficulty understanding the tape; yet, to Tan, her mother's English is perfectly clear and vivid. This difference in understanding helps Tan realize that she, as well as her mother, are affected by the way they use language. Tan then describes two incidents in which her mother suffered prejudicial treatment because of her "limited" English.

When writing, Tan imagines a particular audience—her mother. Tan learns to write not only a "simple" English, the language she spoke to her mother, but also a "broken" English, the language her mother uses with her, and a "watered down" English, the translation of her mother's Chinese into English. Tan calls the "watered down" English an "internal" language—the essence of her mother's intent, passion, imagery, rhythms of speech, and nature of thoughts.

READING/CRITICAL THINKING STRATEGIES

Expressing an Opinion

Before students begin their reading, introduce them to the idea of "Englishes" by asking them to discuss their ideas of "good" and "bad" English. In addition, ask them to discuss the various dialects of English that they are familiar with. Encourage students to think about the varieties of English they speak and under what circumstances they speak them. What kinds of English do they most enjoy reading? What kinds do they most enjoy writing? Tell students to pay careful attention to the attitudes that Tan expresses toward English. You may want to encourage students to map their findings. After students have finished their reading, ask them to share their findings and to express their opinions of Tan's attitudes.

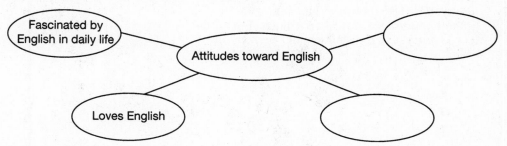

continued ☞

ANSWER KEYS

READING CHECK

A. 1. F   4. F
      2. T   5. T
      3. T

B. Answers will vary. Suggested responses appear below.
   1. Tan defines herself only as a writer, not as an English or literature scholar. She loves language.
   2. One of the two incidents of prejudice in the essay concerns a stockbroker who delayed sending her check. The other concerns a hospital employee who lost a medical test result and was unwilling to look for it.
   3. Tan's Englishes are: 1) "simple"—the English she used with her mother; 2) "broken"—the English her mother used with her; 3) "watered down"—Tan's translation of Chinese into English; and, 4) her mother's internal language—her own translation if she spoke perfect English
   4. Her mother is her best critic because her mother understands all of her languages.

STUDY GUIDE

1. Because she loves language
2. She was giving a speech in very formal English. Her mother, who had never heard Tan use such formal language, was in the audience.
3. Language fascinates her and she spends a lot of time thinking about it.
4. Tan says her mother's English is limited, broken, or fractured.
5. Because of her limited use of English, Tan's mother was viewed by others as someone with limited importance. Yes, as a teenager, Tan let her mother's English affect her perception of her.

6. She would have to imagine an associative situation.
7. Interpretations will vary, but students should include Tan's four definitions of English because they are based on her mother's understanding of the language. There should also be a statement about the student's understanding of the last paragraph.

LANGUAGE SKILLS

A. 1. Amy Tan writes that sometimes she speaks formal English, and sometimes she says things like, "Not waste money that way." (*Page 923*)
   2. Her essay, "Mother Tongue," points out some of the difficulties Asian students have with English.
   3. She tells of making phone calls for her mother. She writes, "I had to get on the phone . . . and say, 'This is Mrs. Tan.'"
   4. After studying Chinese literature, I wrote a poem about China titled "Summer in Shanghai."
   5. In "Mother Tongue," Amy Tan explains her success in mastering English this way: "Fortunately, I happen to be rebellious in nature and enjoy the challenge of disproving assumptions made about me." (*Page 926*)

B. 6. isn't   11. she's
      7. father's   12. China's
      8. he'll   13. essay's
      9. banks'   14. daughter's
     10. boss'   15. shouldn't

Reading Check

Amy Tan   *Mother Tongue*   *(Page 922)*

─────────────── **READING CHECK** ───────────────

A. True/False. Write **T** for a true statement. Write **F** for a false statement.

_____ 1. After Tan played the tape of her
           mother telling a story, not one
           of her friends understood her
           mother's language.

_____ 2. Tan says that she uses different
           Englishes in different situations.

_____ 3. Tan's mother suffered prejudicial
           treatment because she spoke broken
           English.

_____ 4. Tan was an excellent English
           student and scored very high
           on all of her English achieve-
           ment tests.

_____ 5. Tan thinks that Asian American
           students study engineering
           more often than language
           because the former is more
           precise.

B. **1.** How does Tan define herself?

_____

_____

_____

2. What two incidents of prejudice did Tan's mother experience?

_____

_____

_____

3. List and define Tan's four Englishes.

_____

_____

_____

4. Who is Tan's best critic? Why?

_____

_____

Study Guide

Amy Tan (1952–) MOTHER TONGUE *(Page 922)*

Understanding the Writer and Her Background

1. Why did Tan start writing fiction?

_____

_____

Understanding the Selection

2. Under what circumstance did Tan become "keenly aware of the different Englishes" she used?

_____

_____

_____

3. What is Tan's attitude about language?

_____

_____

4. How does Tan describe her mother's English?

_____

_____

5. Why did Tan's mother receive prejudicial treatment from others? Was Tan ever prejudiced against her mother in the same way?

_____

_____

_____

_____

continued ☞

NAME _____

CLASS _____ DATE _____

6. When presented with an analogy in school, how was Tan able to understand the relationships being compared?

_____

_____

_____

Writing and Responding to Literature

7. Write an essay comparing Tan's attitude toward her mother and language. Be sure to include explanations of all of Tan's Englishes. How do they relate to her mother? What is the significance of the last paragraph? Use evidence from the essay to support your comments.

_____

_____

_____

_____

_____

_____

_____

_____

_____

_____

_____

_____

_____

_____

_____

_____

_____

Language Skills

Mother Tongue   **Amy Tan**   *(Page 922)*

———— QUOTATION MARKS, APOSTROPHES, ITALICS ————

As you read this excerpt from Amy Tan's "Mother Tongue," notice the use of the quotation marks, apostrophes, and italics. Quotation marks here are used to set off a direct quotation, apostrophes are used to show where letters have been omitted in contractions, and italics are used to indicate the title of a book.

> But it wasn't until 1985 that I finally began to write fiction. And at first I wrote using what I thought to be wittily crafted sentences, sentences that would finally prove I had mastery over the English language. Here's an example from the first draft of a story that later made its way into *The Joy Luck Club,* but without this line: "That was my mental quandary in its nascent state." A terrible line, which I can barely pronounce.   *(Page 926)*

Quotation Marks

In addition to setting off direct quotations, **quotation marks** are used to enclose titles of short works, such as short stories, poems, essays, articles, songs, and chapters and other parts of books.

> EXAMPLE   Amy Tan wrote "Mother Tongue" about her different ways of using English.

Quotation marks are also used to enclose slang words, invented words, technical terms, and dictionary definitions.

> EXAMPLE   And this makes me think that there are other Asian-American students whose English spoken in the home might also be described as "broken" or "limited."
> *(Page 926)*

Use single quotation marks to enclose a quotation within a quotation.

> EXAMPLE   Amy Tan writes about her mother, "Here's what she said in part: 'Du Yusong having business like fruit stand. Like off the street kind. He is Du like DuZong—but not Tsung-ming Island people.'"   *(Page 923)*

ACTIVITY A

In the following sentences, add single or double quotation marks where they are needed.

1. Amy Tan writes that sometimes she speaks formal English, and sometimes she says things like, Not waste money that way.

2. Her essay, Mother Tongue, points out some of the difficulties Asian students have with English.

3. She tells of making phone calls for her mother. She writes, I had to get on the phone . . . and say, This is Mrs. Tan.

continued ☞

4. After studying Chinese literature, I wrote a poem about China titled Summer in Shanghai.

5. In Mother Tongue, Amy Tan explains her success in mastering English this way: Fortunately, I happen to be rebellious in nature and enjoy the challenge of disproving assumptions made about me. *(Page 926)*

Apostrophes

Apostrophes are used in contractions to show where letters, words, or numbers have been omitted.

EXAMPLES	I am	I'm
	they are	they're
	he is	he's
	was not	wasn't
	1995	'95
	there is	there's

In addition to their use in contractions, apostrophes are used to show the possessive case of a noun or a pronoun.

To form the possessive of a singular noun, add an apostrophe and an *s.*

EXAMPLE   Later, the gangster became more powerful, far richer than my mother's family, ...   *(Page 923)*

To form the possessive of a plural noun ending in *s,* add only the apostrophe.

EXAMPLE   Amy Tan wrote a novel about mothers' and daughters' relationships.

ACTIVITY B

On the lines provided, form contractions or the possessive case of the following words as indicated.

6. is not (contraction) _____

7. father (possessive) _____

8. he will (contraction) _____

9. banks (possessive) _____

10. boss (possessive) _____

11. she is (contraction) _____

12. China (possessive) _____

13. essay (possessive) _____

14. daughter (possessive) _____

15. should not (contraction) _____

continued ☞

NAME _____

CLASS _____ DATE _____   LANGUAGE SKILLS—CONTINUED

Italics

Use italics (underlining, if handwritten or typewritten) for titles of books, plays, periodicals, news-papers, works of art, films, television programs, long musical compositions, trains, ships, aircraft, and spacecraft.

    EXAMPLE   Amy Tan wrote a best-selling novel called *The Joy Luck Club.*

ACTIVITY C

On the lines provided, rewrite the following sentences, adding quotation marks, apostrophes, and italics (*or* underlining) as needed.

16. Amy Tan had her own mothers life and language in mind when she wrote both Mother Tongue and The Joy Luck Club.

_____

_____

_____

17. Tans novel was made into a movie, The Joy Luck Club, in 1993.

_____

_____

_____

18. In Mother Tongue, Tans description of sentence completion problems, such as, Even though Tom was _____, Mary thought he was _____., are humorous.

_____

_____

_____

19. Tan learned, she says, . . . I should envision a reader for the stories I would write.

_____

_____

_____

20. We hope shes going to write many more essays, stories, and novels.

_____

_____

_____

TEACHER'S NOTES

THE NAMES OF WOMEN *Louise Erdrich* Text Page 928

OBJECTIVES

The aims of this lesson are for the student:
- To understand the significance of names in the Anishinabe culture
- To analyze Erdrich's use of details
- To trace the general history and meaning of a name

INTRODUCING THE SELECTION

Louise Erdrich, American short story writer, novelist, and poet, writes about her Native American heritage. One of her strengths lies in her ability to create a strong sense of place.

Her husband, who is also part Native American, is very involved in her career. With his experience as a literary collaborator and anthropologist, he is able to help her talk out plot lines and characterization. He also is her agent.

Erdrich has always enjoyed a strong familial support system. When she was a child, her father would pay her a nickel for each story she wrote. Then her mother would weave together strips of construction paper to make book covers. So at an early age, Erdrich found herself to be a published author earning royalties. In this fun, creative environment, her parents instilled in her an appreciation for reading and writing, an attitude that motivates her still.

SUMMARY

Louise Erdrich describes the importance of what's left of the Anishinabe culture by explaining the importance of names, which, she says, "tell stories, or half stories, if only we listen closely." After describing the meanings of numerous Anishinabe women's names, Erdrich parallels the loss of identities with the loss of names (the French gave the Anishinabe Christian names). Yet these people, especially the women, were sturdy, hard-working, and lucky. The luckiest women, such as both of Erdrich's great-grandmothers, acquired carts.

One of her great-grandmothers, Elise Eliza McCloud, used her cart when peddling her hand-made tourist items in North Dakota. Her other great-grandmother, Virginia Grandbois, who lived to be very old, had a strong, willful personality. Once Virginia decided that she wanted to be in her own home, she tried to walk there—over a hundred miles away. Erdrich associates her great-grandmother's urge to return home with her own urge to write.

Erdrich does not make quilts, can food, grow food, gather herbs and berries, or prepare buffalo hides like her great-grandmothers did. She carries on these traditions by writing them down—by creating a written record of what once was life for Anishinabe women when these women "wore names that told us who they were."

READING/CRITICAL THINKING STRATEGIES

Making Inferences

Before students begin their reading, ask them to discuss names that have special connotations for them. Allow students to consider place names as well as names for people. What intrigues them about these names? With students, read through the first paragraph and the line that follows it and then ask them to predict what they will find in the essay. Tell students to consider what the women of the past mean to the author. Ask students to pause at least five times in their reading to make notes about the inferences they have drawn. Students might record their notes on a chart like the one on page 96. After students have completed their reading, ask them to discuss their findings and to arrive at agreement about what the women of the past mean to the author. Encourage students to discuss their reactions to Erdrich's work.

continued ☞

Inference	Evidence
She would like to know the stories of the women whose names she lists.	She invents stories based on the names of her people.

VOCABULARY

The following words are defined in the glossary:

ecclesiastical   (929)   liaison   (931)   slough (s)   (931)

ANSWER KEYS

READING CHECK

A. 1. F   4. T
   2. T   5. T
   3. F

B. 1. Anishinabe, woman
   2. They lost their identities.
   3. It is her urge to write, to find her own identity in her writing.
   4. She is the first in a long line of women to not rely on the earth for survival. She is first not to save the autumn's harvest in a cellar. She records practices rather than participates in them.

STUDY GUIDE

1. She focuses on how the parts of oneself war against each other within the person.

2. It was considered presumptuous, unbecoming, vain.
3. They married French trappers and farmers.
4. Their Indian identities were lost.
5. She tied her to a chair and the chair to the wall.
6. She is not bound by Anishinabe traditions and customs.
7. Interpretations will vary, but students should mention that "home" to Erdrich is writing. That is where she finds her identity.

SELECTION TEST

1. d   3. d   5. b   7. b   9. d
2. d   4. c   6. a   8. b   10. b

Louise Erdrich *The Names of Women* *(Page 929)*

READING CHECK

A. True/False. Write **T** for a true statement. Write **F** for a false statement.

_____ 1. "The Names of Women" is fiction.

_____ 2. Louise Erdrich is a member of the Turtle Mountain Chippewas of North Dakota.

_____ 3. The Anishinabes did not speak their own names because the names were sacred.

_____ 4. If a woman had a cart she was considered lucky.

_____ 5. Erdrich is the first in a long line of women who will not rely on the earth for survival.

B. 1. From what language is *ikwe*? What does it mean?

_____

2. What happened to the identities of the women when they were given Christian names?

_____

_____

3. Explain Erdrich's "urge to get home."

_____

_____

4. How is Erdrich's life different from all of her mothers' lives?

_____

_____

_____

_____

_____

_____

Louise Erdrich (1954–)   THE NAMES OF WOMEN   *(Page 928)*

Understanding the Writer and Her Background

1. What is the focus of Erdrich's writing?

_____

_____

_____

Understanding the Selection

2. Why didn't the Anishinabe say their own names?

_____

_____

3. Who did the Anishinabe mix with and marry?

_____

_____

4. After the first tribal roll, the Anishinabe were given Christian names. What was the result?

_____

_____

5. How did her daughter keep Virginia Grandbois from walking home over a hundred miles away?

_____

_____

6. Why is Erdrich free to do whatever feels right?

_____

_____

continued ☞

NAME _____

CLASS _____ DATE _____

Writing and Responding to Literature

7. Erdrich describes her great-grandmother Virginia Grandbois' effort to get home. Write an essay explaining the way(s) Erdrich's "urge to get home" is similar to her great-grandmother's? Use evidence from the story to support your comments.

_____

_____

_____

_____

_____

_____

_____

_____

_____

_____

_____

_____

_____

_____

_____

Louise Erdrich   The Names of Women

(Page 929)

Directions: Write the letter of the *best* answer to each question. *(10 points each)*

1. How is Erdrich's life different from all of her mothers' lives?
   a. She is the first in a long line of women free from having to rely on the earth for survival.
   b. She is the first not to save the autumn's harvest in a cellar.
   c. She records traditional practices rather than participates in them.
   d. All the above.   1. _____

2. The woman who could see things moving far across the lake was named
   a. Sounding Feather
   b. Prairie Chicken
   c. Ice
   d. Standing Across   2. _____

3. According to the Anishinabe, to say one's own name was considered
   a. presumptuous
   b. unbecoming
   c. vain
   d. all the above   3. _____

4. The Anishinabe, who were given Christian names by the French, lost their
   a. ponies
   b. land
   c. identities
   d. carts   4. _____

5. The very lucky Anishinabe women acquired
   a. ponies
   b. carts
   c. land
   d. husbands   5. _____

6. Among all the Anishinabe women in "The Names of Women," Erdrich discusses two who were of particular personal importance. They were her
   a. great-grandmothers
   b. great aunts
   c. sisters
   d. none of the above   6. _____

7. Virginia Grandbois' "entire life, her hard-won personality, boiled down in the end to one stubborn, fixed, desperate idea." What was that idea?
   a. She wanted a cart.
   b. She wanted to go home.
   c. She wanted a daughter.
   d. She wanted to plant her squash seeds.   7. _____

continued ☞

NAME _____

CLASS _____ DATE _____   SELECTION TEST—CONTINUED

8. *Ikwe* in Anishinabe language means
   a. man
   b. woman
   c. child
   d. home   8. _____

9. Erdrich writes about people
   a. from dual cultures
   b. with mixed parentage
   c. with complex identities
   d. all the above   9. _____

10. Erdrich's writing focuses on
   a. cultural and social issues
   b. how parts of an individual war against themselves within the person
   c. spiritual practices versus earth-centered practices
   d. none of the above   10. _____

UNIT ASSESSMENT STRATEGIES

UNIT TESTS   The assessment tools provided with this program include **Mastery Tests, Analogy Tests,** and **Composition Tests**. These tests, covering materials in this section, are found on the pages that follow the **Teacher's Notes**. Answer Keys for these tests begin below.

ALTERNATE OR PORTFOLIO ASSESSMENT   Since students vary widely in their aptitude and learning styles, this program provides evaluation tools for a broad range of assessment strategies. The forms and guidelines in this program provide rubrics for you to use in assessing compositions or for student or peer-group evaluation of compositions.

In addition to the unit tests described above, here is a list of other evaluation or assessment tools that are in the program:

- **Student Learning Options**—These suggested unit projects are listed on the unit interleaf pages in the *Annotated Teacher's Edition*.
- **Suggestions for Portfolio Assessment Projects**—This list of possible projects for student portfolios is located in the *Portfolio Assessment and Professional Support Materials* booklet.
- **Fine Arts and Instructional Transparencies**—These transparencies reinforce concepts covered in the unit. The transparencies are accompanied by Teacher's Notes and blackline masters with writing skills. The transparencies for each unit are located in the *Audiovisual Resource Binder*.
- **Evaluation Guides**—These forms are helpful for revising and assessing student papers, whether by you as instructor, by the student, or by peer evaluators. See the *Portfolio Assessment and Professional Support Materials* booklet.

For a variety of assessment and evaluation suggestions, see the *Portfolio Assessment and Professional Support Materials* booklet.

ANSWER KEYS

MASTERY TEST

Modern Nonfiction

A. 1. b   4. a
    2. c   5. d
    3. b

B. For Composition

Guidelines for Essay Topic

In a well-written essay on this topic, the student should

1. Reflect an accurate understanding of the assignment
2. Recognize this theme as occurring in all of the three basic nonfiction forms, citing at least one author from each of the groups:

- Essay
  —E. B. White (humorous comment on destruction of the natural world of Thoreau)
  —James Baldwin (a more serious critical essay on literature as humanizing effort)
- Speech
  —William Faulkner (a most eloquent plea for the survival of man)
  —Rolando R. Hinojosa-Smith (the importance of place)
- Biography
  —John Dos Passos (sketch of Henry Ford)
  —Autobiographies of Zora Neale Hurston, Thomas Wolfe, Richard Wright, and N. Scott Momaday—all dealing with their very human experiences

continued ☞

3. Support all generalizations with details from the works of the several authors used as evidence

4. Demonstrate effective use of the following writing skills:
   - Vocabulary
   - Mechanics (spelling/punctuation/grammar)
   - Sentence structure
   - Organization (logical arrangement of ideas)

ANALOGY TEST

1. —B— cryptic : enigmatic :: exterminate : eliminate
Both pairs are synonyms.

2. —B— intervene : intercede :: inter : bury
Both pairs are synonyms.

3. —C— benign : harmless :: steadfast : enduring
Both pairs are synonyms.

4. —A— resolve : decide :: reject : repudiate
Supersede and supplant are synonyms meaning to solve. Reject and repudiate are synonyms meaning to refuse to accept or support.

5. —D— fidelity : loyalty :: honesty : integrity
Both pairs are synonymous nouns.

6. —B— extol : laud :: decry : belittle
To extol is to laud or praise. To decry is to belittle, tear down, run down, or depreciate. Both pairs are synonymous verbs.

7. —E— grandiloquent : ordinary :: irresolute : decisive
A grandiloquent speech is very flowery and ornate, which is the opposite of ordinary. Irresolute is the opposite of decisive. Both pairs are antonyms.

8. —B— enmity : amity :: deletion : insertion
Both pairs are antonyms. Enmity (hostility) is the opposite of amity (friendliness). A deletion (omission) is the opposite of an insertion.

9. —A— ostracize : banish :: falsify : alter
These pairs are synonyms.

10. —C— churchly : ecclesiastical :: elaborate : ornate
The pairs are synonymous adjectives.

11. —E— caper : escapade :: complaint : grievance
Both pairs are synonyms.

12. —B— nomadic : sedentary :: integral : unnecessary
Nomadic (migratory, wandering) is the opposite of sedentary (not migratory). These pairs are antonyms.

13. —E— nocturnal : diurnal :: safe : dangerous
Nocturnal and diurnal are antonyms meaning night and day. Safe and dangerous have this same relationship.

14. —A— banality : originality :: boredom : excitement
Both pairs are antonyms.

15. —D— wean : addict :: upbraid : praise
To wean (separate, withdraw) is the opposite of to addict. To upbraid (scold) is the opposite of to praise.

16. —B— usurp : power :: plunder : goods
To usurp means to take power, position, or property and hold by force. To plunder means to deprive of goods or property by violence.

17. —E— verity : prevarication :: ambiguity : clarity
Both pairs are antonyms.

18. —A— inauspicious : unpropitious :: bracing : refreshing
Both pairs are synonyms.

19. —C— congenial : harmonious :: antipathetic : belligerent
These pairs are synonyms.

20. —D— disconsolate : cheerful :: torrid : impassive
Both pairs are antonyms.

COMPOSITION TEST

Student answers will vary, but students should write a composition response that has coherence and unity and that adequately covers the topic selected. Students should select a topic from among the choices given, express their opinions clearly in accordance with materials that they have read, and support their ideas with quotations or specific details from the selections. You may want to have students evaluate one another's compositions in cooperative groups. For assessment, you may wish to use one of the array of evaluation guides in the *Portfolio Assessment and Professional Support Materials* booklet.

Mastery Test

MODERN NONFICTION

(Pages 865–933)

A. Understanding Nonfiction. Read the following excerpt, and then answer the questions that follow. (*8 points each*)

> I now saw a world leap to life before my eyes because I could explore it, and that meant not going home when school was out, but wandering, watching, asking, talking. Had I gone home to eat my plate of greens, Granny would not have allowed me out again, so the penalty I paid for roaming was to forfeit my food for twelve hours. I would eat mush at eight in the morning and greens at seven or later at night. To starve in order to learn about my environment was irrational, but so were my hungers. With my books slung over my shoulder, I would tramp with a gang into the woods, to rivers, to creeks, into the business district, to the doors of poolrooms, into the movies when we could slip in without paying, to neighborhood ball games, to brick kilns, to lumberyards, to cottonseed mills to watch men work. There were hours when hunger would make me weak, would make me sway while walking, would make my heart give a sudden wild spurt of beating that would shake my body and make me breathless; but the happiness of being free would lift me beyond hunger, would enable me to discipline the sensations of my body to the extent that I could temporarily forget.
>
> —Richard Wright, *Black Boy**

1. In the above passage, all of the following facts are clear *except* one. Which is the exception?
   a. The narrator's family was very poor.
   b. The narrator had many brothers and sisters.
   c. His grandmother was an authority figure.
   d. His experiences in the outside world were limited.

   1. _____

2. The overriding reality of the narrator's life and motives at this time clearly involved, above all else,
   a. a sense of loneliness   **c.** a variety of hungers
   b. an escape from tyranny   **d.** trusted new friends

   2. _____

3. The narrator did not go home after school but roamed instead so that he could
   a. run away   **c.** rebel
   b. learn   **d.** loaf

   3. _____

4. The narrator's adventures brought him mainly a sense of
   a. freedom   **c.** self-expression
   b. independence   **d.** self-confidence

   4. _____

continued ☞

5. The after-school activities that the narrator treasured involved his
   a. family   **c.** sense of maturity
   b. escape from Granny   **d.** fascinating experiences   **5.** _____

B. **For Composition.** American writers who have emerged since World War I represent a variety of styles and personalities, yet they have been united in "their opposition to the dehumanizing elements in a mechanized world and in their effort to affirm the dignity of human beings in an increasingly grim and ambiguous time." Comment on this statement, citing evidence from the nonfiction selections in this unit.

MODERN NONFICTION

Analogies. For each question, choose the lettered pair which expresses a relationship that is most similar to that of the capitalized pair.

QUESTION 1. _____
CRYPTIC : ENIGMATIC ::
A. tomblike : joyous
B. exterminate : eliminate
C. epigraphic : epigrammatic
D. inscribed : ominous
E. solar : geothermal

QUESTION 2. _____
INTERVENE : INTERCEDE ::
A. intend : stop
B. inter : bury
C. ignore : meddle
D. interact : enact
E. scream : whisper

QUESTION 3. _____
BENIGN : HARMLESS ::
A. blithe : starry
B. constant : variable
C. steadfast : enduring
D. whimsical : steady
E. fickle : sober

QUESTION 4. _____
RESOLVE : DECIDE ::
A. reject : repudiate
B. provide : deny
C. offend : compliment
D. accept : resign
E. extend : curtail

QUESTION 5. _____
FIDELITY : LOYALTY ::
A. subway : submarine
B. fiction : nonfiction
C. suburb : city
D. honesty : integrity
E. underground : aviation

QUESTION 6. _____
EXTOL : LAUD ::
A. resolve : complicate
B. decry : belittle
C. blame : praise
D. venerate : condemn
E. eulogize : pan

QUESTION 7. _____
GRANDILOQUENT : ORDINARY ::
A. eloquent : articulate
B. passionate : ardent
C. monthly : yearly
D. austere : measured
E. irresolute : decisive

QUESTION 8. _____
ENMITY : AMITY ::
A. sender : transmittal
B. deletion : insertion
C. caper : escapade
D. sympathy : understanding
E. aversion : disaffection

QUESTION 9. _____
OSTRACIZE : BANISH ::
A. falsify : alter
B. ignore : repudiate
C. eliminate : establish
D. welcome : expatriate
E. displace : deride

QUESTION 10. _____
CHURCHLY : ECCLESIASTICAL ::
A. bland : placid
B. ordinary : unique
C. elaborate : ornate
D. intricate : simple
E. unaffected : affected

continued ☞

QUESTION 11. _____
CAPER : ESCAPADE ::
A. eclipse : display
B. conjunction : divorce
C. umbrella : shadow
D. gravity : velocity
E. complaint : grievance

QUESTION 12. _____
NOMADIC : SEDENTARY ::
A. comic : humorous
B. integral : unnecessary
C. itinerant : vagabond
D. dwelling : abiding
E. aboriginal : native

QUESTION 13. _____
NOCTURNAL : DIURNAL ::
A. null : numeral
B. lunar : insane
C. nocuous : sunny
D. nightly : monthly
E. safe : dangerous

QUESTION 14. _____
BANALITY : ORIGINALITY ::
A. boredom : excitement
B. trite : verbose
C. pithy : lucid
D. common : pedestrian
E. hackneyed : overused

QUESTION 15. _____
WEAN : ADDICT ::
A. shrink : reduce
B. detach : replace
C. admire : idolize
D. upbraid : praise
E. tantalize : tease

QUESTION 16. _____
USURP : POWER ::
A. surprise : astonishment
B. plunder : goods
C. reconstruct : age
D. surrender : despair
E. inject : sleep

QUESTION 17. _____
VERITY : PREVARICATION ::
A. vernacular : dialect
B. training : preparation
C. authenticity : reality
D. writing : words
E. ambiguity : clarity

QUESTION 18. _____
INAUSPICIOUS : UNPROPITIOUS ::
A. bracing : refreshing
B. favorable : adverse
C. benign : malignant
D. auxiliary : concentric
E. delicious : insipid

QUESTION 19. _____
CONGENIAL : HARMONIOUS ::
A. friendly : ornery
B. mismatched : compatible
C. antipathetic : belligerent
D. generous : selfish
E. congenital : defective

QUESTION 20. _____
DISCONSOLATE : CHEERFUL ::
A. isolated : separated
B. querulous : grouchy
C. undiplomatic : arrogant
D. torrid : impassive
E. poised : stately

Composition Test

MODERN NONFICTION *(Pages 865–933)*

A. One of the themes that emerges from study of modern American nonfiction is a concern with the writer's own development as a creative artist. Examine the experience of any *two* of the following writers: James Baldwin, Richard Wright, Rolando R. Hinojosa-Smith. In your essay, focus on the elements that the individual writers consider formative.

B. Analyze the use of irony in "Walden (June 1939)" (page 867) and "Tin Lizzie" (page 895).

_____
_____
_____
_____
_____
_____
_____
_____
_____
_____
_____
_____
_____
_____
_____
_____
_____
_____
_____

continued ☞

_____

_____

_____

_____

_____

_____

_____

_____

_____

_____

_____

_____

_____

_____

_____

_____

_____

_____

_____

_____

_____

_____

TEACHER'S NOTES

UNIT 7: Modern Drama

UNIT OBJECTIVES

The aims of this unit are for the student:

- To analyze the works of three major authors from modern drama: Glaspell, O'Neill, and Wilder
- To identify and explain the purpose behind the unusual staging and theatrical techniques, evident in all three plays included in the textbook, but especially in *Our Town*
- To explain in what sense Mrs. Wright is tried by her peers
- To identify and explain characteristic concerns and themes of O'Neill as found in *Where the Cross is Made*
- To demonstrate an understanding of the major themes in *Our Town*, especially the connection between individual lives and Nature's striving for perfection
- To write a composition agreeing or disagreeing with Wilder's ideas about nature, as expressed in *Our Town*, and a composition comparing the theme of overlooking life's seemingly insignificant details in *Our Town* and in *Trifles*
- To write an essay or dramatic sketch that presents a cross section of people in the students' home towns

OVERVIEW OF THE UNIT

The history of drama, dating from the ceremonial "goat plays" of ancient Greece, has been long and varied. For Aristotle, drama was "imitated human action." Perhaps people have always gone to the theater to obtain a view of their own complex actions. Drama is a means by which we investigate our problems or laugh at our follies. Plays are particularly popular with students because of their dramatic episodes, their vivid characters, and the opportunity they provide for active participation—if not as an "actor," at least as a viewer or reader.

The three plays in this unit—Susan Glaspell's *Trifles*, Eugene O'Neill's *Where the Cross is Made*, and Thornton Wilder's *Our Town*—will provide students with a well-rounded introduction to American drama.

ANSWER KEYS

STUDY GUIDE

1. Answers will vary.
2. *Tragedy* focuses on an individual who struggles against impossible odds but ultimately cannot control the overwhelming forces working against him; it does not end happily. *Comedy* does have a happy ending; the follies of human nature are expressed but do not present insurmountable obstacles to the characters' well-being.
3. Scenery, costumes, body movement, and lighting
4. Ibsen wrote plays that deal with common problems of ordinary life, thus bringing to the theater a new focus on *realism*. Strindberg is known for exploring psychological reality, the characters' inner feelings—a development called *expressionism*.
5. **a.** a struggle or clash that a main character experiences. It might be with other characters, external forces, or his inner self.
   b. the main character in a play
   c. conversation; spoken words
   d. a movement in drama to explore the mind or inner reality of the characters
6. Answers will vary. Students might note that dramatists must be more concise, must confine the action to fewer people and settings, and must capitalize on visual aspects of staging.

SELECTION TEST

A.
1. d	7. c
2. a	8. b
3. d	9. b
4. c	10. b
5. b	11. a
6. d	12. d

B.
13. c	15. a
14. b	16. b

Study
Guide

MODERN DRAMA

Introduction *(Pages 934–939)*

1. Aristotle defined drama as "an imitation of an action." In your own words, tell what that means.

_____

_____

_____

2. Identify the two main kinds of drama and briefly describe each one.

_____

_____

_____

_____

_____

_____

3. A written play is different from its staged version. Identify four aspects of staging which can influence audience perception and understanding.

_____

_____

4. Both Henrik Ibsen and August Strindberg made important contributions to modern drama. Explain what each is known for.

_____

_____

_____

_____

_____

continued ☞

5. Briefly define each of the following terms:

    a. conflict _____

    _____

    _____

    b. protagonist _____

    _____

    _____

    c. dialogue _____

    _____

    _____

    d. expressionism _____

    _____

    _____

6. The first paragraph of the introduction states that dramatists "recognize that they must tell their stories in a different way from novelists." What are some of these differences?

_____

_____

_____

_____

_____

_____

_____

_____

_____

Selection
Test

MODERN DRAMA

Introduction   *(Pages 934–939)*

A.   Understanding Drama. Write the letter of the *best* answer to each question. *(5 points each)*

1. The word *drama* comes from a Greek word meaning
   a. "to imitate"
   b. "to show"
   c. "to recognize"
   d. "to do"

   1. _____

2. More than 2,000 years ago, Aristotle defined drama as "an imitation of an _____."
   a. action
   b. interesting crisis
   c. important person
   d. art form

   2. _____

3. According to Aristotle's definition, a play's plot must nearly always involve a
   a. setting
   b. plot
   c. crisis
   d. conflict

   3. _____

4. The main character's decision to perform or not to perform some morally meaningful act leads to the play's
   a. moment of crisis
   b. scene of suspense
   c. resolution
   d. explanation

   4. _____

5. Traditionally, drama has been categorized under two main types,
   a. farce and realism
   b. comedy and tragedy
   c. spectacle and vaudeville
   d. pantomine and didacticism

   5. _____

6. Comedy is basically concerned with which of the following?
   a. A simple protagonist
   b. Two antagonists
   c. Unreasonable ambitions
   d. Human vices and follies

   6. _____

7. A typical pair of comic protagonists might be a
   a. young man and an older man
   b. child and a parent
   c. young couple
   d. young woman and an older woman

   7. _____

8. The basic "bricks and mortar" of every drama is its
   a. main character
   b. dialogue
   c. plot
   d. conflict

   8. _____

9. The "other language" of a play, what Aristotle called "spectacle," is
   a. resolution
   b. staging
   c. lighting
   d. movement

   9. _____

10. What kind of play would need no scenery, costume, gesture, movement, or lighting?
    a. A television comedy
    b. A radio play
    c. An experimental play
    d. An expressionistic play

    10. _____

continued ☞

11. When *reading* a play silently, what helps the reader to imagine
the playwright's staging?
   a. Stage directions   c. Lighting cues
   b. The cast of characters   d. Costuming directions   11. _____

12. What did Aristotle mean by "imitation"?
   a. An exact reproduction of real life
   b. A life-size performance
   c. An artificial copy
   d. A reenactment of common experiences   12. _____

B. The Development of American Drama. Write the letter of the *best* answer to each
question. *(10 points each)*

13. The main types of nineteenth-century drama in America were
   a. tragedy and realism   c. melodrama and farce
   b. realism and expressionism   d. comedy and farce   13. _____

14. The two dramatists who laid the groundwork for twentieth-century realism
and expressionism are
   a. Shakespeare and Sheridan   c. Aristophanes and Sophocles
   b. Ibsen and Strindberg   d. Wilde and Shaw   14. _____

15. A "slice-of-life" play asks the audience to accept the stage as
   a. an ordinary room with one wall removed
   b. an outward expression of the mind
   c. an all-purpose area with or without scenery
   d. a representation of a particular level of society   15. _____

16. Realism and expressionism first became important in the American theatre
with the plays of
   a. Thornton Wilder   c. Arthur Miller
   b. Eugene O'Neill   d. Tennessee Williams   16. _____

TEACHER'S NOTES

TRIFLES *Susan Glaspell* Text Page 940

OBJECTIVES

The aims of this lesson are for the student:
- To identify details that unravel the murder mystery
- To interpret in what sense Mrs. Wright is tried by her peers
- To describe the County Attorney's attitude toward women
- To write a composition analyzing the women's decision to conceal the dead bird

INTRODUCING THE SELECTION

An early feminist, Susan Glaspell keenly felt the double standards and injustices that her turn-of-the-century, male-dominated society imposed and committed upon women. As her play *Trifles* illustrates, Glaspell believed that men generally treated the women in their lives as frivolous, even simple-minded, children. Happily, Glaspell's own marriage to George Cram Cook proved to be a partnership of two equally creative and energetic people.

Trifles, her most famous one-act play, is similar in form to Glaspell's numerous other works. Glaspell excelled at focusing on one moment—one slice of life—and revealing it with clarity and precision to an audience. It may be worthwhile to discuss with students how Glaspell's work as a newspaper reporter may have influenced her perceptions and her writing style.

Another point to note is the subtle but persuasive argument that Glaspell introduces first in this play and then emphasizes in the ironic title of her short story "A Jury of Her Peers," which is based on the play. Simply put, Glaspell asserts that men and women are not, and perhaps cannot be, "peers." Therefore, to judge Mrs. Wright's actions by a male code of law is an injustice. Certainly, the idea shocked audiences in Glaspell's time and may well spark useful debate in today's classroom.

SUMMARY

The scene of this play is the farmhouse kitchen of John and Minnie Wright. Lewis Hale and Sheriff Peters have brought the county attorney to the house where Hale had discovered Mr. Wright's dead body the day before. Mrs. Wright has been arrested for her husband's murder. While the men search for clues to her motives, Mrs. Peters and Mrs. Hale look over the unkempt house, which Mrs. Hale says was always cheerless. She also reveals that Wright was "a hard man." The women discover a bird cage in a cupboard and later find a dead canary hidden in a box. They realize that Mrs. Wright killed her husband just as he had strangled the canary and the joy out of her own life during the thirty years of their marriage. Because the two women sympathize with Mrs. Wright, they hide the bird and keep quiet.

READING/CRITICAL THINKING STRATEGIES

Drawing Conclusions

As a prereading strategy, ask students to discuss mystery stories that they have enjoyed. You may also want to ask them to discuss favorite detectives from film or television. Tell students that the story they are about to read involves a mystery and tell them that as they read they should consider the clues as to "whodunit" and why. Students might note clues in a chart like the one on page 117. After students have completed their reading, ask them to share their findings and to determine who committed the murder and why. Do students agree that Mrs. Peters and Mrs. Hale have made the right decision?

continued ☞

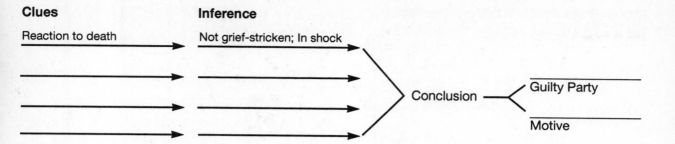

Clues	Inference
Reaction to death	Not grief-stricken; In shock

Conclusion — Guilty Party

Motive

VOCABULARY ACTIVITY

To create dialogue that sounds natural and realistic, playwrights often interject nonstandard words and usage into the speech of their characters. In *Trifles*, Glaspell uses this technique to catch the authentic sound of conversation between farmers and rural folk.

Point out to the class two or three instances of nonstandard usage in the play; examples are found in Mr. Hale's speech on page 942 ("ain't," "set [rather than sit] down," "kind o' dull like," "rockin'," and "then I says.") Then ask your students to find additional examples throughout the rest of the play.

As the students identify examples, ask them who is speaking. Write the name of each character on the chalkboard and put a mark below the appropriate name each time an example is given. After students have gone through the entire play and found all the examples they can, total the number of marks under each name and identify which characters use nonstandard English most frequently. (When determining these totals, be sure to remind students to consider the number of examples of nonstandard English in light of how large a speaking role the character has.)

Finally, lead the class in exploring how differences in the use of nonstandard English contribute to characterization in *Trifles*. You might point out, for example, that Mr. Hale uses proportionally more nonstandard English than do the other characters and that such usage makes him sound less educated and sophisticated than the others.

ANSWER KEYS

STUDY GUIDE

1. She was a journalist. She got the idea for *Trifles* from an experience she had while working as a reporter.

2. She and her husband organized a theater group called the Provincetown Players, which performed plays by Eugene O'Neill and others.

3. Possible examples include: (1) "I don't think a place'd be any cheerfuller for John Wright's being in it" (p. 944); (2) "Wright was close," made his wife feel shabby (p. 944); (3) "he was a hard man . . ." (p. 947); and (4) He was "no company when he did come in" (p. 946).

4. Possible answers: (1) men can be patronizing and unsympathetic to women's drudgery and isolation; (2) the "lowly" women in the play—not the men with their official titles—have the wits to uncover what has happened; (3) a woman can be completely stifled by her miserly, unsociable husband.

5. Mrs. Wright "was kind of like a bird herself—real sweet and pretty, but kind of timid and—

fluttery." She also used to sing, but "he killed that, too." Thus Mr. Wright not only killed the bird, but also the elements in his wife that resembled the bird. Seen as a victim, Mrs. Wright gains our sympathy for any subsequent actions she might have taken.

6. If Mrs. Wright was indeed the murderer, she probably used the rope to strangle her husband just as he strangled the bird.

7. Answers will vary, but students should note the title's irony.

8. Answers will vary. Students might suggest that there is enough evidence to indict, but that extenuating circumstances might justify an acquittal. Students' answers should include evidence that supports their position.

LANGUAGE SKILLS

A. 1. had, wanted   4. looks
   2. was   5. was
   3. wanted

continued ☞

B. 6. I asked her why I couldn't see him.

7. Harry said that he was dead all right.

8. I asked whether anybody had been notified.

9. She said that she didn't know.

10. She said that she didn't wake up.

C. Answers may vary slightly; possible answers are provided.

11. Mrs. Hale said that there's a great deal of work to be done on a farm.

12. Mrs. Hale asked Mrs. Peters whether she thought Mrs. Wright had done it.

13. Mrs. Peters told Mrs. Hale that the law is the law.

14. Mrs. Peters asked Mrs. Hale what she was doing.

15. Mrs. Hale said that she had known John Wright.

BUILDING VOCABULARY

A. Answers will vary slightly.

1. "How do you do, Mrs. Wright. It is cold, isn't it?"

2. "No," she said gloomily.

3. "He was hanged."

4. "We must have appeared confused."

5. "I suppose it is."

6. "We must not be upset."

B. Examples will vary. Some possibilities are:

7. NONSTANDARD ENGLISH "Chill out." "Be cool." STANDARD ENGLISH "Relax."

8. NONSTANDARD ENGLISH "I'm gonna ace that test." STANDARD ENGLISH "I am going to do well on that test."

9. NONSTANDARD ENGLISH "That's bad." "That's awesome." STANDARD ENGLISH "That is very good."

SELECTION TEST

1. c	3. d	5. c	7. d	9. d
2. a	4. b	6. d	8. b	10. b

Susan Glaspell (1882–1948)

TRIFLES *(Pages 940–949)*

Understanding the Writer and Her Background

1. What was Glaspell's occupation before she turned to writing fiction? How did that

   career lead to *Trifles*? _____

   _____

   _____

2. How did Glaspell help give exposure to the works of other dramatists? _____

   _____

   _____

Understanding the Selection

3. John Wright was apparently not a very likeable man. Locate four statements which sway
   the audience against Mr. Wright and keep us from sympathizing with him even though
   he is the victim.

   _____

   _____

   _____

   _____

   _____

4. Identify at least three feminist themes or attitudes expressed in the play.

   _____

   _____

   _____

   _____

5. How is Mrs. Wright linked closely to the bird? What is the dramatic effect of creating

that link? _____

_____

_____

_____

_____

_____

6. There was apparently a gun in the house, yet it wasn't used in the murder. How does
the use of a rope instead of a gun serve to implicate Mrs. Wright?

_____

_____

_____

_____

7. How would you explain the play's title?

_____

_____

_____

Writing and Responding to Literature

8. As a member of a grand jury, would you vote to indict Mrs. Wright on the basis of the
evidence presented in the play? As a jury member, would you vote to convict her?
Explain your answers.

_____

_____

_____

_____

_____

Language
Skills

Trifles *Susan Glaspell* *(Page 941)*

———————————— INDIRECT QUOTATIONS ————————————

Sometimes writers want to report what a person said without using the speaker's exact words. This type of reporting is often used to provide background information. As you read the following excerpt, notice how the character Hale provides background by summarizing past conversations.

> **Hale.** . . . I spoke to Wright about it once before and he put me off, saying folks talked too much anyway, and all he asked was peace and quiet—I guess you know about how much he talked himself; but I thought maybe if I went to the house and talked about it before his wife, though I said to Harry that I didn't know as what his wife wanted made much difference to John—
> *(Page 942)*

Indirect quotations do not include quotation marks. Notice that the verb in an indirect quotation may be in a tense different from the one the speaker used.

EXAMPLES   I said to Harry <u>that I didn't know</u>. . . .   **[Indirect quotation]**

I said to Harry, "<u>I don't know.</u>"   **[Direct quotation]**

A verb in an indirect quotation usually has the same tense as the main verb in the sentence (*said/didn't*). Notice also that an indirect quotation frequently forms a subordinate clause introduced by *that* (*said that, says that, asked that,* etc.).

ACTIVITY A

Write the correct form of the bracketed verb, making the verb tense in the indirect quotation match the tense of the main verb in the sentence.

1.   . . . I said I [have] _____ come in to see if John [want]

_____ to put in a telephone. . . .   *(Page 943)*

2. I dunno, maybe it wasn't scared. I wouldn't like to say it [be] _____.
    (Page 943)

3. She said she [want] _____ an apron.   *(Page 944)*

4. Mr. Peters says it [look] _____ bad for her.   *(Page 945)*

5. Mr. Henderson said coming out that what [be] _____ needed for the case was a motive. . . .   *(Page 945)*

continued ☞

ACTIVITY B

Change these direct quotations to indirect quotations. Do not change the tense of the main verb.

> EXAMPLE   . . . I said, "I want to see John." *(Page 942)*
>
> I said that I wanted to see John.

6. "Then why can't I see him?" I asked her. . . . *(Page 942)*

_____

7. . . . Harry . . . said, "No, he's dead all right. . . ." *(Page 942)*

_____

8. "Has anybody been notified?" I asked. *(Pages 942–943)*

_____

9. "I don't know," she says. *(Page 943)*

_____

10. "I didn't wake up," she said. . . . *(Page 943)*

_____

ACTIVITY C

Change these lines from the play to indirect quotations.

> EXAMPLE   **County Attorney.** And how did she—look? *(Page 942)*
>
> The County Attorney asked how she had looked.

11. **Mrs. Hale** *(stiffly)*.   There's a great deal of work to be done on a farm. *(Page 943)*

_____

_____

12. **Mrs. Hale.**   [to Mrs. Peters] Do you think she [Mrs. Wright] did it? *(Page 945)*

_____

_____

continued ☞

13. Mrs. Peters.   But, Mrs. Hale, the law is the law.   *(Page 945)*

_____

_____

14. Mrs. Peters.   Oh, what are you doing, Mrs. Hale?   *(Page 946)*

_____

_____

15. Mrs. Hale.   I knew John Wright.   *(Page 948)*

_____

_____

Building Vocabulary

Susan Glaspell *Trifles* *(Page 941)*

———— REVISING NONSTANDARD ENGLISH INTO STANDARD ENGLISH ————

Nonstandard language is usage that is limited to a particular region, group, or situation. To create dialogue that sounds natural and realistic, playwrights often interject nonstandard words and usage into the speech of their characters. In *Trifles,* Susan Glaspell uses this technique to catch the authentic sound of conversation between farmers and rural folk.

ACTIVITY A

The following excerpts are examples of nonstandard words and usage found in *Trifles*. Read each excerpt and rewrite it in standard English.

1. "How do, Mrs. Wright, it's cold, ain't it?"

   _____

   _____

2. " 'No,' she says, kind o' dull like."

   _____

   _____

3. "He died of a rope around his neck."

   _____

   _____

4. "We must 'a looked as if we didn't see how that could be. . . ."

   _____

   _____

5. "I s'pose 'tis."

   _____

   _____

6. "We mustn't take on."

   _____

   _____

continued ☞

ACTIVITY B

Now, think about the way people speak in the area where you live. Write examples of nonstandard English that might be heard in your school or neighborhood. Rewrite each example, using standard English.

NONSTANDARD   I'm fixin' to go to the library.
STANDARD   I'm getting ready to go to the library.

NONSTANDARD   Traffic was slow due to all the rubberneckers.
STANDARD   Traffic was slow because of all the curious passersby who found it necessary to turn their heads and take a look.

7. NONSTANDARD ENGLISH _____

_____

STANDARD ENGLISH _____

_____

8. NONSTANDARD ENGLISH _____

_____

STANDARD ENGLISH _____

_____

9. NONSTANDARD ENGLISH _____

_____

STANDARD ENGLISH _____

_____

Selection Test

Susan Glaspell *Trifles*

(Pages 940–949)

Directions: Write the letter of the *best* answer to each question. *(10 points each)*

1. An important character who never appears on stage is
   a. George Henderson
   b. Henry Peters
   c. Minnie Wright
   d. Lewis Hale

   1. _____

2. John Wright might be described as all of the following *except*
   a. talkative
   b. stingy
   c. cruel
   d. cheerless

   2. _____

3. The outcome of the play can be termed ironic because
   a. Mrs. Wright cares more about her preserves than her husband's death
   b. the men don't understand women
   c. the women don't understand their husbands
   d. the women hide the evidence the men need to convict Mrs. Wright

   3. _____

4. According to the County Attorney, what important fact is missing in this murder case?
   a. The cause of death has not been determined.
   b. There is no apparent motive.
   c. There isn't a likely suspect.
   d. There are no eyewitnesses to testify.

   4. _____

5. Which of the following is *not* an accurate description of the County Attorney's attitude toward women?
   a. He is demeaning.
   b. He is patronizing.
   c. He respects their concerns.
   d. He expects women to be loyal to their sex.

   5. _____

6. A number of details in the play gain sympathy for Mrs. Wright. Which of the following is *not* one of them?
   a. The men belittle Mrs. Wright's anxiety about her preserves.
   b. Mrs. Hale recalls that in her youth Minnie Foster was pretty and lively.
   c. The Wright farm is described as lonesome and depressing.
   d. The County Attorney shows little interest in the apron or quilt pieces.

   6. _____

7. The two women uncover all of the following pieces of incriminating evidence *except* a
   a. badly sewn quilt block
   b. broken birdcage
   c. dead bird
   d. dirty roller towel

   7. _____

8. Even though Mrs. Wright did not ask for this item, Mrs. Hale thought it was important to send her
   a. a bible
   b. a jar of her preserves
   c. a loaf of her bread
   d. quilt pieces

   8. _____

continued ☞

9. The climax of the play occurs when
  a. Mrs. Hale rips out the sewing in the quilt
  b. Mrs. Peters finds a birdcage
  c. the two women discover the dead bird
  d. Mrs. Hale conceals the box

  9. _____

10. An important theme in the play is the
  a. shortcomings of the legal system
  b. importance of seemingly trivial details of life
  c. need for sympathy and understanding
  d. superiority of emotion over reason

  10. _____

TEACHER'S NOTES

WHERE THE CROSS IS MADE   *Eugene O'Neill*   Text Page 950

OBJECTIVES

The aims of this lesson are for the student:
- To identify and explain characteristic concerns and themes of O'Neill as found in *Where the Cross Is Made*
- To write a composition discussing various meanings of the word *cross* in O'Neill's play

INTRODUCING THE SELECTION

Eugene O'Neill was born to the theater, but he was nearly thirty before he began to approach drama with the intentness of purpose that was to make him the greatest American playwright of his time.

As a child, O'Neill often toured with his father, the famous James O'Neill, best known for his acting in *The Count of Monte Cristo* and, as an alternate to Edwin Booth, in the role of Othello. As a youth, Eugene himself played for a time in *The Count of Monte Cristo*, but his performance satisfied neither his father nor himself. His schooling, as might be expected, was irregular. When unsettled behavior and lack of study led to his dismissal from Princeton after one year, he entered upon a period of restlessness during which he worked briefly for a New York mail-order firm, traveled to Honduras to seek gold, and then joined the crew of a Norwegian steamer on its way to Buenos Aires, where he worked in the offices of American business firms. Before long, he was a seaman on the New York–to–Southampton route. This five-year period of rootlessness, brought to an abrupt end by a six-month hospitalization for tuberculosis in 1912–1913, furnished him with background experience which he utilized in his plays.

O'Neill is perhaps best known for two kinds of plays. On the one hand, he wrote experimental works such as *The Emperor Jones* (1920), *The Great God Brown* (1926), *Strange Interlude* (1928), and *Mourning Becomes Electra* (1931). On the other hand, there are his naturalistic tragedies, often rendered in four acts, like *The Iceman Cometh* (1946), *A Moon for the Misbegotten* (1947), *Long Day's Journey into Night* (1956), and *A Touch of the Poet* (1957). However, O'Neill began as a writer of one-act plays—for example, *Thirst* (1914), *Bound East for Cardiff* (1916), and *The Moon of the Caribbees* (1918). His skill in this form is well illustrated by the present selection, *Where the Cross is Made*.

The relation of one-act plays to full-length plays is similar to the relation of short stories to novels. Resembling the short story, the one-act play stresses unity of effect, which may be defined as the creation of a single mood through character, plot, setting, and dialogue. When assigning *Where the Cross Is Made*, you could ask the students to determine what mood is being evoked and how the author has evoked it. You may wish to direct your students' attention to the Commentary on page 962, which deals in part with the playwright's use of expressionistic devices to create and sustain a mood.

SUMMARY

This somber, one-act drama is set in a house on the California coast on a windy fall night in 1900. Nat Bartlett, a gaunt, thirty-year-old writer, is arranging to commit his father, a sea captain, to an asylum. Against all reason, Captain Bartlett constantly watches for his ship to return with the treasure he had discovered and buried years before. Nat claims that his father is mad because he denies that his ship was wrecked years ago. Nat and his sister argue over what to do with their father. Blaming his father for the loss of his right arm, Nat burns his copy of the treasure map. The captain appears and says that his ship has returned. Pushed beyond his limit, Nat falls apart and joins in his father's fantasy. When the captain dies of heart failure, Nat pledges to continue the search to find the treasure.

continued ☞

Making Inferences About Fantasy and Reality

As a prereading strategy, ask students to define illusion and delusion and to discuss the connotations of each word. (It is not necessary for students to make a clear distinction; rather, they should understand that both involve a failure to distinguish fantasy from reality.) Tell students that the characters in *Where the Cross is Made* find it difficult to distinguish fantasy from reality. Ask students to consider what each character's illusions and delusions are. After students have completed their reading, ask them to discuss their findings. Do they see any connections between the characters' fantasies? What role do they think illusions/delusions play in establishing the theme of the play?

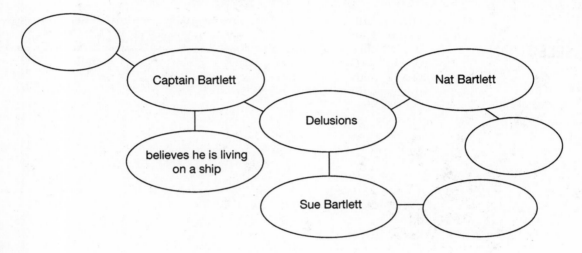

VOCABULARY   The following words are defined in the glossary:

winnow (ed)	(951)	**perfunctory (–ily)**	(954)	**transfigure (d)**	(959)
sallow	(952)	**supplicate (–ingly)**	(956)	**sinewy**	(960)
unkempt	(952)	**vindictive (ly)**	(956)	**matted**	(960)
sardonic (ally)	(954)	**placate (–ingly)**	(958)		

ANSWER KEYS

STUDY GUIDE

1. His father was a famous actor; thus, O'Neill grew up in and around the theater.
2. He spent time at sea, working on a ship.
3. He emphasized realism in his plays but also tried to present the "inner reality" of his characters through the use of dreams, masks, and monologues.
4. Nat hates his father for forcing him into a life at sea, which claimed his arm, yet is completely dominated by him and unable to throw off the psychological yoke.

5. Possible examples include: (1) the ship was definitely determined to be sunk; (2) the jewels were paste; (3) the "ship" and "crew" he saw were not really there; and (4) he turned the house into a ship.
6. Examples might include: (1) the apparitions which Nat and his father see but Sue doesn't; (2) the green lighting near the end; and (3) Nat's destroying the map to "destroy" the madness inside him.

continued 🖙

7. Students' answers will vary, but should include the following points. With Higgins, Nat speaks in complete, fully coherent, and logically connected sentences. Later his speech is disjointed; ideas are left dangling and are interrupted by frequent exclamations. The breakdown of his speech patterns reflects the internal breakdown he undergoes.

LANGUAGE SKILLS

A. 1. only touch of color
   2. pale
   3. blue
   4. wistful
   5. fading
   6. twilight gray
   7. low
   8. melancholy

B. 9. madness
   10. sane, asylum, poisonous, save, soul

C. 11. role, plot, scenery, monologue
   12. spoken, dialect, decipher, narrative
   13. duty, shift, retire, promotion

D. 14.–21. Answers will vary.

BUILDING VOCABULARY

Answers will vary.

SELECTION TEST

1. b	3. b	5. d	7. d	9. c
2. c	4. c	6. b	8. c	10. d

Study Guide

Eugene O'Neill (1888–1953)

WHERE THE CROSS IS MADE *(Pages 950–962)*

Understanding the Writer and His Background

1. In what way was O'Neill "born to the theater"?

_____

_____

2. What experience as a young man gave O'Neill material for this play?

_____

_____

3. What innovations did O'Neill bring to the American theater?

_____

_____

_____

Understanding the Selection

4. Briefly describe the relationship between Nat and his father.

_____

_____

_____

5. How does the audience know that the Captain is truly mad?

_____

_____

_____

_____

Understanding Literary Elements

6. *Expressionism* was defined in the unit introduction as an "attempt to show psychological reality." Give three examples of expressionistic devices in the play.

_____

_____

_____

_____

_____

_____

Writing and Responding to Literature

7. Look at Nat's language in the early part of the play when he talks to Dr. Higgins. Contrast it with his manner of speech toward the end, after his father appears. How does the change reflect Nat's mental state?

_____

_____

_____

_____

_____

_____

_____

_____

Language Skills

Where the Cross Is Made   *Eugene O'Neill*   *(Page 951)*

———————————— CONNECTIONS BETWEEN IDEAS ————————————

Successful writers choose words carefully to help the reader make connections between ideas. As you read the following excerpt, notice the repeated words.

> **Nat.**   . . . Smith said he would give two thousand cash if I would sell the place to him—and he would let me stay, rent-free, as a caretaker.
>
> **Sue** *(scornfully).*   Two thousand! Why, over and over the mortgage it's worth—
>
> **Nat.**   It's not what it's worth. It's what one can get, cash—for my book— for freedom!   *(Page 956)*

Eugene O'Neill reminds the reader of ideas already mentioned by repeating key words like *two-thousand, cash,* and *worth.* He also connects ideas by using other words closely related to the topic: *sell, rent-free,* and *mortgage.* A third way to connect ideas is by using the synonym for a word mentioned earlier: *money* for *cash* or *value* for *worth,* for example.

ACTIVITY A

Read the following passage from the stage directions. Then in the blanks below, list eight words or phrases that reinforce the idea of Sue's being "pale" and "sad," as described in the first sentence.

> She is a tall, slender woman of twenty-five, with a pale, sad face framed in a mass of dark red hair. This hair furnishes the only touch of color about her. Her full lips are pale; the blue of her wistful wide eyes is fading into a twilight gray. Her voice is low and melancholy. She wears a dark wrapper and slippers. *(Page 955)*

1. _____

2. _____

3. _____

4. _____

5. _____

6. _____

7. _____

8. _____

continued ☞

ACTIVITY B

Read the following passage and answer the questions that follow it.

Sue. . . . Nat! Don't! You talk as if—

Nat. . . . As if I were mad? You're right—but I'll be mad no more! See! (*He . . . sets fire to the map. . . .*) See how I free myself and become sane. And now for facts, as the doctor said. I lied to you about him. He was a doctor from the asylum. See how it burns! It must be destroyed—this poisonous madness. . . . Yes, I sold him, if you will—to save my soul. They're coming from the asylum to get him— *(Page 958)*

9. Although Nat appears to be concentrating on the map, what is the real topic of this excerpt?

_____

10. Put an **X** beside the words below that reinforce this topic.

_____ free   _____ sane   _____ facts   _____ lied

_____ asylum   _____ poisonous   _____ save   _____ soul

ACTIVITY C

Put an **X** beside the words in each column that are related to the topic given at the top of the column.

11. <u>Drama</u>

_____ role

_____ pronoun

_____ plot

_____ retire

_____ scenery

_____ monologue

12. <u>Language</u>

_____ shield

_____ spoken

_____ dialect

_____ retire

_____ decipher

_____ narrative

13. <u>Employment</u>

_____ duty

_____ dream

_____ shift

_____ retire

_____ example

_____ promotion

continued ☞

ACTIVITY D

Select one of the following topics and circle it. In the blanks, write words related to this topic that you might use when writing a paragraph on it.

TOPICS	music	collecting	family life	friendship	tests

14. _____

15. _____

16. _____

17. _____

18. _____

19. _____

20. _____

21. _____

NAME _____

CLASS _____ DATE _____ SCORE _____

Eugene O'Neill *Where the Cross Is Made* (Page 951)

———— FINDING DEFINITIONS, SYNONYMS, AND ANTONYMS ————

ACTIVITY

Eugene O'Neill uses the words listed below in *Where the Cross Is Made.* Choose four words from the list. Look up the definitions of these words in the glossary in the textbook and at least one dictionary. Write the words you chose and a definition for each of them. Next, list three words or phrases that are **synonyms,** or have a similar meaning. Then list three words or phrases that are **antonyms,** or have an opposite meaning. Finally, write an original sentence, using each of the words as you have defined it.

hysterically	perfunctory	sardonically	vindictively
indefinitely	placate	sinewy	

1. WORD _____

DEFINITION _____

SYNONYMS (3) _____

ANTONYMS (3) _____

ORIGINAL SENTENCE _____

_____

2. WORD _____

DEFINITION _____

SYNONYMS (3) _____

ANTONYMS (3) _____

ORIGINAL SENTENCE _____

_____

continued ☞

3. WORD _____

DEFINITION _____

SYNONYMS (3) _____

ANTONYMS (3) _____

ORIGINAL SENTENCE _____

_____

4. WORD _____

DEFINITION _____

SYNONYMS (3) _____

ANTONYMS (3) _____

ORIGINAL SENTENCE _____

_____

Selection Test

Eugene O'Neill   *Where the Cross Is Made*

(Pages 950–962)

Directions: Write the letter of the *best* answer to each question. *(10 points each)*

1. *Where the Cross Is Made* contains all of the following *except*
   a. the sea as a pervasive presence
   b. a character who functions as chorus
   c. a troubled relationship between father and son
   d. the tension between reality and illusion

   1. _____

2. Nat Bartlett considers his father to be all of the following *except*
   a. quite mad
   b. an ignorant sailor
   c. a dangerous maniac
   d. a victim of his own delusions

   2. _____

3. In what length of time does all the action in the play take place?
   a. In about four years
   b. In a single night
   c. In one day and one evening
   d. In two successive evenings

   3. _____

4. The world long inhabited by both Nat and his father is a world of
   a. confident expectations
   b. patient waiting
   c. dreams and illusions
   d. quarreling and accusations

   4. _____

5. The play's plot involves all of the following *except*
   a. a shipwreck
   b. a buried treasure
   c. drowned seamen
   d. an onstage death

   5. _____

6. The Captain's "cabin" and "ship's deck" symbolize his
   a. lost hopes
   b. withdrawal from normal human life
   c. power and authority
   d. sense of humor

   6. _____

7. Who is involved in the plot to place the Captain in an insane asylum?
   a. Nat only
   b. Dr. Higgins only
   c. Nat and Sue
   d. Nat and Mr. Smith

   7. _____

8. The set design and lighting of the play have the effect of
   a. making the action subordinate to mood
   b. emphasizing the romantic nature of the sea
   c. merging the land and the water
   d. creating an atmosphere of tranquillity

   8. _____

9. Which of the following does *not* help bring on the Captain's death?
   a. Joy over the return of his ship and its three seamen
   b. Anger over his son's treacherous plans
   c. Realization that he is mad and there is no ship
   d. The prospect of being placed in an insane asylum

   9. _____

continued ☞

10. This short play contains elements of all the following *except*

   a. melodrama   **c.** expressionism

   b. realism   **d.** an unhappy romance   **10.** _____

OUR TOWN   *Thornton Wilder*   Text Page 963

OBJECTIVES

The aims of this lesson are for the student:
- To identify and explain the purpose behind the unusual staging and theatrical techniques used in *Our Town*, and to demonstrate an understanding of how these fit into the play's themes
- To demonstrate an understanding of the major themes in *Our Town*, especially the connection between individual lives and Nature's striving for perfection
- To write a composition agreeing or disagreeing with Wilder's ideas about nature, as expressed in *Our Town*, and a composition comparing the theme of overlooking life's seemingly insignificant details in *Our Town* and in *Trifles*

INTRODUCING THE SELECTION

"The real genius of *Our Town*, says Rex Burbank (in his book *Thornton Wilder* [Twayne Publishers, 1961]), "consists in Wilder's success in making the ordinary interesting to watch and in portraying the intrinsic value without falling into bathos."

As your class will quickly notice, there is nothing terribly exciting about Joe Crowell's delivering the paper, Wally Webb's eating his breakfast, Howie Newsome's covering his milk route, or Mrs. Webb's determination to can forty quarts of string beans even "if it kills me." It is the audience's—or the reader's—early realization that the daily trivialities somehow carry a larger meaning that gives the play its suspense, low-keyed though it may be.

One doesn't ever feel safe when generalizing about high-school students, but it may be possible to assert two general notions relevant to a discussion of *Our Town*. (1) Students are more attracted to the confraternity of the theater than to dramatic literature as such. As a place full of ropes, scratched floors, wobbly sets, and role-playing, the theater is exciting, marked with the chalk of glamour and fame. More as a way of life than as an art form, the theater exerts a pull toward adventure and boldness. (2) Students are terrified of ambiguity, especially ambiguity of motive; they will back off from anything or anyone that they suspect of "putting them on."

If you have a class which seems to respond well to making plays "work," you may wish to involve the class in an oral reading. *Our Town* can be performed readily in a classroom, and almost everybody can take part if you reassign the roles for each act.

On the other hand, you might wish merely to assign the play as reading matter and defer the major part of the discussion until it is time to deal with the play as a whole. The role of the Stage Manager and the function of plot, character, and setting can be discussed after a complete reading of the play.

Be sure to refer your students to the Commentary that follows each act of *Our Town*, textbook pages 980, 994, and 1003.

SUMMARY

This play presents a probing but affectionate look at life's universal concerns and cycles. A folksy narrator, the Stage Manager, presides over various scenes in a small town called Grover's Corners in New Hampshire. Act One suggests the ordinary daily life of the town in 1901, focusing on the families of Doc Gibbs and Editor Webb. Act Two takes place three years later and is about the love and marriage of teenagers George Gibbs and Emily Webb. Act Three, set nine years later, takes place in the cemetery on the day of Emily's funeral. Before taking her place among the dead, Emily begs to relive one happy day. She finds the experience painful because the living are "blind" to the richness of life. The narrator says there is something eternal about every human being, and he stresses the cyclical and universal nature of human experience.

continued ☞

READING/CRITICAL THINKING STRATEGIES

Expressing an Opinion

Before students begin their reading, ask them to discuss what they think daily life in the United States was like in 1901. Then, encourage students to discuss whether they think the changes that have occurred since that time have made major changes in our values and beliefs. Tell students to make note of any differences that they see between lifestyles in 1901 and current lifestyles. Students should also note any changes that they see in values and beliefs. After students have finished their reading, ask them to compare their findings. What are the most significant differences between 1901 and today? Does anything remain basically unchanged?

Similarities	Differences
Churches	No cars
Public school	Doctor makes house calls

Expressing an Opinion

Before students begin their reading, ask them to consider how the following people are likely to react when involved in a wedding: the bride, the groom, the father of the bride, the mother of the bride, and father of the groom, the mother of the groom. Tell students to consider whether each of the characters (the bride, the groom, etc.) reacts in the way they expected. After students have completed their reading, ask them to discuss their findings and to discuss why their predictions proved valid or invalid.

Making Inferences About Theme

Before students begin their reading, you might ask them to consider what they think may be true of human life at any place and at any given time. Do students believe that there are universal human truths? If so, what are they? Tell students to consider whether Wilder believes that such truths exist. If so, what are they? You might encourage students to note any references to the ideas of time, eternity, and truth. After students have completed their reading, ask them to share their findings. What does Wilder believe about universal truths? How do students react to his beliefs?

References to Time ⟶	Inference
"and then time . . . sunny days"	Path easy with time

References to Eternity ⟶	Inference

References to Truth ⟶	Inference

continued ☞

VOCABULARY The following words are defined in the glossary:

Act One		*Act Two*		*Act Three*	
highboy	(970)	pantomime (s)	(984)	lugubrious (ness)	(995)
legacy	(971)	alacrity	(985)	genealogist (s)	(995)
meteorological	(971)	affront (ed)	(990)	bereave (d)	(996)
precipitation	(971)	sacrament	(990)		
belligerent	(972)	unobtrusive (ly)	(992)		
silicate	(975)	tableau	(993)		

VOCABULARY ACTIVITY

Solving analogies helps students build vocabulary skills by providing practice with categorizing, interpreting context clues, differentiating between shades of meaning, examining relationships between words and concepts, and applying a number of other basic techniques for determining the meaning of unfamiliar words. To help students master unfamiliar words in *Our Town,* present the following incomplete analogies to the class and have students fill in each blank with an appropriate word. If you have identified other words that have given students difficulty, you may wish to create analogies for those words and add them to this list.

1. botanical : flora :: meteorological : _____
2. flour : bread :: silicate : _____
3. illumination : daylight :: affronted : _____
4. belligerent : calm :: unobtrusive : _____
5. bereaved : saddened :: affronted : _____

Answers: [Note: These are possible answers; student answers will likely vary.]

1. weather. Something that is botanical concerns flora; something that is meteorological concerns weather.
2. glass (or brick). Flour is an ingredient in bread; silicate, in glass or brick.
3. rain (or snow). One kind of illumination is daylight; one kind of precipitation is rain or snow.
4. obvious. *Belligerent* is an antonym of *calm; unobtrusive,* of *obvious.*
5. offended. Someone who is bereaved is saddened; someone who is affronted is offended.

ANSWER KEYS

READING CHECK

Our Town, Act One   Text Page 964

A.
1.	T	6.	T
2.	F	7.	T
3.	F	8.	F
4.	F	9.	T
5.	T	10.	F

B. Answers will vary. Major events include: Mrs. Gibbs is offered money for their chest of drawers; Emily wants to know if she is pretty; the town is putting memorabilia in a cornerstone; Stimson comes to choir practice drunk again; Dr. Gibbs refuses to travel to Europe with Mrs. Gibbs; Emily has trouble sleeping.

READING CHECK

Our Town, Act Two   Text Page 982

A.
1.	T	6.	F
2.	F	7.	F
3.	T	8.	T
4.	T	9.	F
5.	F	10.	T

continued ☞

B. Answers will vary. Major events in this act do not occur in chronological order, but they include: Emily accuses George of acting "stuck up" and he apologizes; George decides not to go away to college; George and Emily get married.

Our Town, Act Three   Text Page 995

A.
1.	T	6.	F
2.	F	7.	T
3.	T	8.	T
4.	T	9.	F
5.	F	10.	T

B. Answers will vary. Major events include: Emily dies in childbirth; she chooses to go back and relive her twelfth birthday and realizes that she took much in life for granted; George visits her grave; life goes on in Grover's Corners.

Our Town, Acts One–Three   Text Page 964

1. He spent much of his boyhood in China.
2. He tends to explore universal themes and writes in a simple, graceful style.
3. **a.** The Cartwrights are building a new bank (p. 975).
   b. The first car will appear in five years. Doc Gibbs died in 1930. Joe died in the war.
   c. He philosophizes about marriage (p. 990) and about the eternal (p. 996). He says it is everyday concerns about *real* life that belong in the bank cornerstone (p. 975).
   d. He talks to Prof. Willard (p. 971). He thanks the Webbs (p. 986).
   e. He takes the roles of Mrs. Forrest (p. 973), Mr. Morgan, the druggist (p. 987), and the clergyman (p. 993).
4. Possible answers might include these points: (1) Emily wonders if she's pretty; (2) Mrs. Gibbs wishes she could take a real trip; and (3) George and Emily both have pre-wedding nervousness.
5. Possible answers might include these points: (1) Prof. Willard recites the geological and historic record; (2) people sit down to dinner, just as they did in Babylon and will do 1,000 years hence; (3) the openings to Acts II and III; (4) "You're twenty-one. . . . Then whissh! you're seventy"; and (5) the letter addressed to Grover's Corners, N.H., USA, Continent of North America. . . .
6. She learns that the living are too busy to appreciate life itself.
7. **a.** Angry, hostile, quarrelsome

b. Quickly, without any hesitation
c. An agitated tone of voice and angry, withdrawing gestures can indicate that he feels offended.
d. She would move quietly trying not to call attention to herself.
e. They would not sound sad or mournful—perhaps, instead, cheerful and in good spirits.

8. Students might offer the following answers: (1) The play opens with "no curtain" and "no scenery"; (2) various props are imaginary; (3) Mrs. Forrest is "invisible"; (4) Emily and George sit on ladders; and (5) the Stage Manager sits on stage "watching the audience return to its seats" before Act II.
9. Answers will vary. The bare minimum of scenery and props serves to emphasize the general over the particular, to reinforce the idea that Grover's Corners is *any* town, that the Gibbs and Webb houses are *any* houses. The staging thus encourages the audience to adapt a detached perspective.
10. The many examples include: (1) "Nobody very remarkable ever come out of it" (p. 966); (2) "Her stummick ain't what it ought to be" (p. 968); (3) "You got to speak to George" (p. 968); (4) ". . . it brung 'em a fortune" (p. 969); (5) "I dunno" (p. 972); (6) "They're all getting citified. . . . They haven't got nothing fit to burgle. . . ." (p. 978–79); and "I don't think he smokes no cigarettes" (p. 979). Students' paragraphs will vary, but they should suggest that the use of colloquial speech makes the characters seem more ordinary, and down-to-earth, in keeping with the ordinariness that unifies the whole play.

Our Town, Acts One–Three   Text Page 964

A.
1. Presently, also
2. first, in fact, there, but, here
3. Since then
4. And now
5. For a while now

B.
6. although
7. However
8. Even though, because
9. however
10. so

C.
11. Often
12. just as
13. Later
14. However
15. Although

continued ☞

VOCABULARY

A. Root meanings are followed by possible
answers for new words.

1. law; legislature
2. war; bellicose
3. holy; sacrifice
4. account or study; biology
5. imitate; mimetic
6. thrust; intrude
7. race or species; genetics

B. 8.–14. Sentences will vary.

SELECTION TEST

A. 1. b   6. c
2. d   7. a
3. c   8. c
4. c   9. b
5. d   10. b

B. 11. d   14. b
12. b   15. d
13. a

Thornton Wilder   *Our Town*

─────────────────────── **READING CHECK** ───────────────────────

Act One

A. **True/False.** Write T for a true statement. Write F for a false statement.

_____ **1.** *Our Town* is set in Grover's Corners, New Hampshire.

_____ **2.** The first act opens at nightfall.

_____ **3.** Howie Newsome is the town's mail carrier.

_____ **4.** Rebecca and Wally are brother and sister.

_____ **5.** Emily helps George with his math.

_____ **6.** For years, Mrs. Gibbs has wanted to visit Paris.

_____ **7.** Dr. Gibbs scolds George for not chopping wood for his mother.

_____ **8.** George wants to be a professor of history at the state university some day.

_____ **9.** Simon Stimson, the church organist, has a drinking problem.

_____ **10.** The first act ends with George and Emily talking about the address on an envelope.

B. List the major events in Act One in the order in which they occurred.

_____

_____

_____

_____

_____

_____

_____

_____

_____

_____

_____

Thornton Wilder *Our Town* (Page 982)

———————————————— **READING CHECK** ————————————————

Act Two

A. True/False. Write T for a true statement. Write F for a false statement.

_____ 1. Act Two of *Our Town* shows the marriage of George and Emily.

_____ 2. Emily has been elected president of her class.

_____ 3. After high school, George plans to go on to agricultural college.

_____ 4. Emily tells George about the flaws in his character.

_____ 5. On the morning of the wedding, George goes over to Emily's house and finds her eating breakfast.

_____ 6. Mr. Webb tells George how he achieved a happy marriage by following his father's advice.

_____ 7. George faces his wedding day with confidence.

_____ 8. Just before the wedding ceremony, Emily says she hates George.

_____ 9. Mrs. Gibbs talks through the wedding ceremony.

_____ 10. The Stage Manager plays the part of the minister at the wedding.

B. List the major events in Act Two in the order in which they occurred.

_____

_____

_____

_____

_____

_____

_____

_____

_____

_____

_____

Reading Check

Thornton Wilder   *Our Town*   *(Page 995)*

──────────────────── **READING CHECK** ────────────────────

Act Three

A. True/False. Write T for a true statement. Write F for a false statement.

_____ **1.** The funeral in Act Three is for Emily.

_____ **2.** Also dead are Mr. and Mrs. Webb.

_____ **3.** Some Civil War veterans are buried in a local cemetery.

_____ **4.** Mr. Webb's son died of appendicitis.

_____ **5.** Emily is happy to leave her life on earth.

_____ **6.** Emily and George have had three children.

_____ **7.** Simon Stimson is bitter about his earthly life.

_____ **8.** For his epitaph, Stimson has no verse, only some musical notes.

_____ **9.** George seems unmoved by his wife's death.

_____ **10.** Mrs. Soames says that life was awful and wonderful.

B. List the major events in Act Three in the order in which they occurred.

_____

_____

_____

_____

_____

_____

_____

_____

_____

_____

_____

Thornton Wilder (1897–1975)

OUR TOWN *(Pages 963–1004)*

Understanding the Writer and His Background

1. What was unusual about Wilder's youth? _____

_____

2. Identify two characteristics of Wilder's writings. _____

_____

Understanding the Selection

3. The Stage Manager is clearly an unusual character. Find examples in the play where he

    a. gives the audience information about current happenings in the town. _____

    _____

    _____

    b. gives the audience information about future occurrences. _____

    _____

    c. injects his own attitude or philosophy. _____

    _____

    _____

    d. as himself interacts with other characters. _____

    _____

    e. in the role of someone else interacts with other characters. _____

    _____

    _____

4. There is not much action in *Our Town*. Instead, the audience is caught up in the very ordinary wishes and fears and worries that the characters reveal. What are three of these?

_____

_____

_____

_____

_____

_____

_____

5. There are numerous instances in which the audience is led to view the particular goings-on in Grover's Corners in the much broader context of universal or cosmic events. Find five such instances.

_____

_____

_____

_____

_____

_____

_____

6. What lesson does Emily learn when she returns from the dead for her twelfth birthday?

_____

_____

_____

_____

Understanding Vocabulary

7. The underlined words given below are used as stage directions to the actors. Checking the glossary as needed, answer each question.

   a. In what tone of voice would the *belligerent* man speak (p. 972)? _____

   _____

   b. How would an actor portraying Mr. Webb respond with *alacrity* (p. 985)?

   _____

   c. How might the Stage Manager show that he is *affronted* (p. 990)? _____

   _____

   d. How would Mrs. Gibbs return *unobtrusively* to her seat (p. 992)? _____

   _____

   e. How would the dead speak so as not to be *lugubrious* (p. 995)? _____

   _____

Understanding Literary Elements

8. The introduction noted the unusual staging of this play. List four specific examples of

   unusual staging. _____

   _____

   _____

   _____

   _____

9. Briefly explain the overall effect of these unorthodox methods. _____

   _____

   _____

   _____

   _____

continued ☞

Writing and Responding to Literature

10. *Our Town* is rich in its use of colloquial speech. Find five examples of informal English in the play, looking for informal vocabulary and pronunciation as well as grammar. Then write a brief paragraph that explains how the use of colloquial speech contributes to the play's effect.

_____

_____

_____

_____

_____

_____

_____

_____

_____

_____

_____

_____

_____

_____

NAME _____

CLASS _____ DATE _____ SCORE _____

Our Town   *Thornton Wilder*   *(Page 964)*

──────────── **TRANSITIONAL EXPRESSIONS** ────────────

Using connectors to show the relationships between ideas helps assure smooth, clear writing. As you read the following two excerpts, notice which words or phrases connect ideas from sentence to sentence or clause to clause.

> **Stage Manager.** . . . The first act was called the Daily Life. This act is called Love and Marriage. There's another act coming after this: I reckon you can guess what that's about. *(Page 982)*

> **Emily.** . . . I used to watch you as you did everything . . . because we'd been friends so long . . . and then you began spending all your time at *baseball* . . . and you never stopped to speak to anybody any more. Not even to your own family you didn't . . . *(Page 987)*

Connectors such as *for instance, although, so, instead,* and *therefore* are called **transitional expressions.** In the first excerpt, Thornton Wilder uses transitional expressions to indicate time: *first, this, another, after this.* In the second excerpt, the word *because* indicates cause or purpose; *then, never,* and *any more* indicate time; and *not even* adds an idea (additional proof of George's "stuck-up" attitude). Transitional expressions may also indicate position (*here, beyond,* etc.), summaries and conclusions (*therefore, in fact,* etc.), and contradiction (*however, yet, but,* etc.).

ACTIVITY A

Circle the transitional expressions in each of the following quotations.

1. Presently the Stage Manager . . . enters and begins placing a table and three chairs downstage left. . . . He also places a low bench at the corner. . . . *(Page 964)*

2. Mrs. Gibbs died first—long time ago, in fact. She . . . died there . . . but her body was brought back here. *(Page 967)*

3. Migration toward the end of the seventeenth century of English brachycephalic blue-eyed stock . . . for the most part. Since then some Slav and Mediterranean— *(Page 972)*

4. There are a hundred and twenty-five horses in Grover's Corners. . . . And now they're bringing in these auto-mobiles. . . . *(Page 988)*

5. In this wedding I play the minister. . . . For a while now, the play gets pretty serious. *(Page 990)*

continued ☞

ACTIVITY B

Circle the transitional expression within brackets that better relates the ideas.

6. The young soldiers buried there had an idea that the Union should be kept together, [because, although] they had never seen more than fifty miles of it themselves.

7. He said he was now in business out in Buffalo. [Consequently, However], he was in Chicago when he got news of his cousin's death.

8. [Even though, Because] she was warned not to go back, Emily insisted [even though, because] she thought she could live her happy days over again.

9. Wilder was not as prolific as other major writers; [however, therefore], he consistently created work of polish and intelligence.

10. The stage manager thinks this play will be good reading a thousand years from now, [but, so] he's going to have a copy of it put in the cornerstone of the new bank.

ACTIVITY C

From the following list of transitional expressions, choose the one that best completes each sentence and write it in the blank.

later   however   although   often   just as

11. Wilder sought to go beneath situations and circumstances peculiar to a specific time.

_____ the underlying ideas are only hinted at.

12. The reader must go beneath this surface, _____ Wilder goes

beneath the surface of everyday life.

13. For seven years Wilder was a housemaster and French teacher at the Lawrenceville

School in New Jersey. _____ he taught at the University of

Chicago and at Harvard University.

14. The stage manager tells the audience, "There's some scenery for those who think

they have to have scenery." _____, scenery is not very important

to the play.

15. _____ Wilder's first novel received little attention, his second

novel, *The Bridge of San Luis Rey*, was hailed as a masterpiece.

Building Vocabulary

Thornton Wilder *Our Town* (Page 964)

———— IDENTIFYING WORD ROOTS / USING WORDS IN CONTEXT ————

The **root** of a word is its core part. Many English words have roots originally derived from Greek or Latin. The word *pompous,* for example, comes from the Latin *pompa,* meaning "display" or "procession." The word *phototropic* is a compound of two Greek roots: *photos* ("light") and *tropos* ("responding to a stimulus"); consequently, a plant that is phototropic is one that responds to light.

ACTIVITY A

The roots of some of the words used by Thornton Wilder in *Our Town* are given below. Look up each word in a dictionary and write the meaning of its Greek or Latin root. Then use the dictionary to locate a new word that contains the same root.

WORD	ROOT	MEANING OF ROOT	NEW WORD
1. legacy	leg	_____	_____
2. belligerent	bell	_____	_____
3. sacrament	sacr	_____	_____
4. meteorological	logos	_____	_____
5. pantomime	mime	_____	_____
6. unobtrusively	trud	_____	_____
7. genealogist	gen	_____	_____

ACTIVITY B

Write original sentences of your own, using each of the new words you wrote in the last column in Activity A.

8. _____

_____

9. _____

_____

continued ☞

10. _____

_____

11. _____

_____

12. _____

_____

13. _____

_____

14. _____

_____

Thornton Wilder   *Our Town*

(Pages 963–1004)

A.   Understanding Drama. Write the letter of the *best* answer to each question. *(6 points each)*

1. In *Our Town,* Wilder focuses on the
   a. dullness of routine, conventional lives
   b. significance of ordinary events
   c. need for change in daily life
   d. excitement of small-town life   **1.** _____

2. The first clue that the Stage Manager is all-knowing is his
   a. statement that the play begins just before dawn
   b. description of the way the town's streets run
   c. reference to the popular grocery store and drugstore
   d. knowledge that the first automobile will be along in five years   **2.** _____

3. A copy of this play will be put in the new bank's cornerstone so that the
   a. name of the town will be perpetuated
   b. future will have an example of an experimental play
   c. real life of the town will be revealed to people of the future
   d. Stage Manager's true role will be preserved for the future   **3.** _____

4. Emily's first moments of worrying involve whether
   a. George likes her   **c.** she is really pretty
   b. she will make a good speech   **d.** George should become a farmer   **4.** _____

5. The play's language is all of the following *except*
   a. essentially simple   **c.** informal
   b. clear   **d.** illiterate, uneducated   **5.** _____

6. The Stage Manager gives the second act of the play a title. It is
   a. "The Daily Life"   **c.** "Love and Marriage"
   b. "The Beginning of Love"   **d.** "The Facts of Life"   **6.** _____

7. In the flashback where George and Emily first knew they were "meant for each other," Emily accuses George mainly of
   a. having become conceited   **c.** being a lazy student
   b. being unkind to others   **d.** playing baseball too much   **7.** _____

8. The dead Simon Stimson insists that to be alive is to be
   a. eternally happy   **c.** ignorant and blind
   b. sad often   **d.** mean and unforgiving   **8.** _____

continued ☞

9. When does Emily realize the difference between the living and the dead?
   a. After a number of years in the grave
   b. Soon after her funeral
   c. When Mrs. Gibbs explains things to her
   d. When the Stage Manager describes the difference   **9.** _____

10. On the day she returns to the living, Emily makes which of the following important discoveries?
   a. People are too concerned with trivial things.
   b. People never realize the value of life while they live it.
   c. People live boring lives.
   d. Life is not what it should be.   **10.** _____

B. **Appreciating the Play as a Whole.** Write the letter of the *best* answer to each question. *(8 points each)*

11. Thornton Wilder's main purpose in using no scenery in *Our Town* was probably to
   a. avoid distracting the audience
   b. save on production costs
   c. give the Stage Manager a more important role
   d. suggest that the town could be anywhere   **11.** _____

12. The Stage Manager contributes to the play's theme and universal application with his
   a. sympathy and patience
   b. complete detachment
   c. willingness to explain things
   d. personal involvement with the other characters   **12.** _____

13. A main theme in the play is that
   a. all people in all ages share common experiences
   b. life on earth is too short
   c. the dead may be happier than the living
   d. love and happiness are very rare   **13.** _____

14. According to the Stage Manager, the only people who understand life may be
   a. elderly husbands and wives   **c.** happy schoolchildren
   b. saints and poets   **d.** the members of a wedding   **14.** _____

15. The Stage Manager's point of view seems to be that
   a. life offers very few choices
   b. people have nothing to look forward to after death
   c. most people lead dull, unhappy lives
   d. life can be rich and happy, and death serene   **15.** _____

UNIT ASSESSMENT STRATEGIES

UNIT TESTS

The assessment tools provided with this program include **Mastery Tests, Analogy Tests,** and **Composition Tests**. These tests, covering materials in this section, are found on the pages that follow the **Teacher's Notes**. Answer Keys for these tests begin below.

ALTERNATE OR PORTFOLIO ASSESSMENT

Since students vary widely in their aptitude and learning styles, this program provides evaluation tools for a broad range of assessment strategies. The forms and guidelines in this program provide rubrics for you to use in assessing compositions or for student or peer-group evaluation of compositions.

In addition to the unit tests described above, here is a list of other evaluation or assessment tools that are in the program:

- **Student Learning Options**—These suggested unit projects are listed on the unit interleaf pages in the *Annotated Teacher's Edition.*
- **Suggestions for Portfolio Assessment Projects**—This list of possible projects for student portfolios is located in the *Portfolio Assessment and Professional Support Materials* booklet.
- **Fine Arts and Instructional Transparencies**—These transparencies reinforce concepts covered in the unit. The transparencies are accompanied by Teacher's Notes and blackline masters with writing skills. The transparencies for each unit are located in the *Audiovisual Resource Binder.*
- **Evaluation Guides**—These forms are helpful for revising and assessing student papers, whether by you as instructor, by the student, or by peer evaluators. See the *Portfolio Assessment and Professional Support Materials* booklet.

For a variety of assessment and evaluation suggestions, see the *Portfolio Assessment and Professional Support Materials* booklet.

ANSWER KEYS

MASTERY TEST

Modern Drama

A. 1. d   4. d
    2. b   5. d
    3. a   6. a

B. 7. b   9. b
    8. b   10. a

C. For Composition
Guidelines

In a well-written essay on this topic the student should:

1. Reflect an accurate understanding of the assignment

2. Take a stand on the question posed: "Is *Our Town* 'soothing'?"

3. Discuss each of the three elements.
   Suggested points are:
   - Tragic strand or theme
     —Simon Stimson's inability to cope with his environment
     —Premature death of Emily
   - Comic moment or theme
     —Folksy humor of individual characters
   - Motif or theme of social criticism
     —Trivial events which become instances of the universal cycle

4. Support all generalizations with details from *Our Town*

continued ☞

5. Demonstrate competence in the following writing skills:
   - Vocabulary
   - Mechanics (spelling/punctuation/grammar)
   - Sentence structure
   - Organization (logical arrangement of ideas)

ANALOGY TEST

1. —C— winnow : harvesting :: sow : planting
   To winnow (scatter, to separate the good from the useless) is part of harvesting. To sow (scatter, plant seeds) is part of planting.

2. —A— sallow : complexion :: equitable : agreement
   Sallow can describe a person's complexion. Equitable can describe an agreement.

3. —E— sardonic : cynical :: identical : interchangeable
   This is a synonym analogy.

4. —A— perfunctory : automatic :: sarcastic : ironic
   Both pairs are synonyms.

5. —E— vindictive : vengeful :: charitable : merciful
   These pairs of words are synonyms.

6. —B— placate : mediator :: judge : arbitrator
   The mediator's task is to placate (calm) the parties in a dispute in order to help bring them to agreement. The arbitrator's task is to listen to the disputing sides and then judge (render a judgment, dictate a settlement).

7. —D— sinewy : muscular :: archaic : obsolete
   Both pairs are synonyms.

8. —C— meteorology : weather :: geology : earth
   Meteorology is concerned with weather. Geology is concerned with the study of the earth.

9. —A— legacy : inheritance :: ancestor : forefather
   Both pairs are synonyms.

10. —D— alacrity : hesitation :: jeopardy : safety
    Alacrity (eager willingness or readiness to act) is the opposite of hesitation (uncertainty, indecision, or reluctance). Jeopardy (danger) is the opposite of safety.

11. —D— affront : offend :: praise : laud
    To affront means to offend. To praise means to laud. Both pairs are synonymous verbs.

12. —A— supplicate : donate :: regard : ignore
    These pairs are opposites. To supplicate is to ask; to donate is to give. To regard is to notice or look at something, instead of ignoring it.

13. —E— precipitation : rain :: mammal : horse
    This is a classification analogy. rain is one form of precipitation. A horse is a type of mammal.

14. —B— unobtrusive : blatant :: tasteful : gaudy
    These pairs are antonyms.

15. —C— unkempt : messy :: shorn : trimmed
    Both pairs are synonyms.

16. —A— belligerent : obedient :: irresolute : determined
    The pairs are antonyms.

17. —C— silicate : glass :: carbon : diamond
    Glass is made from silicates. Diamonds are made from carbon.

18. —E— pantomime : mime :: routine : gymnast
    A mime performs a pantomime. A gymnast performs a routine.

19. —E— transfigure : metamorphose :: meddle : interfere
    Both pairs are synonyms.

20. —B— sacramental : consecrated :: secular : temporal
    Sacramental and consecrated are synonyms meaning holy or sacred. Secular and temporal are synonyms meaning worldly, not spiritual.

COMPOSITION TEST

Student answers will vary, but students should write a composition response that has coherence and unity and that adequately covers the topic selected. Students should select a topic from among the choices given, express their opinions clearly in accordance with materials that they have read, and support their ideas with quotations or specific details from the selections. You may want to have students evaluate one another's compositions in cooperative groups. For assessment, you may wish to use one of the array of evaluation guides in the *Portfolio Assessment and Professional Support Materials* booklet.

MODERN DRAMA

(Pages 934–1004)

A. Understanding Drama. Below is a scene from a play by Eugene O'Neill called *Beyond the Horizon*. Read it, and then answer the questions that follow. *(10 points each)*

Andrew. Here you are, eh?

Robert. Hello, Andy.

Andrew *(going over to Mary)*. And who's this young lady I find you all alone with, eh? Who's this pretty young lady? *(He tickles the laughing, squirming Mary, then lifts her up at arm's length over his head.)* Upsy—daisy! *(He sets her down on the ground again.)* And there you are! *(He walks over and sits down on the boulder beside Robert who moves to one side to make room for him.)* Ruth told me I'd probably find you up topside here, but I'd have guessed it, anyway. *(He digs his brother in the ribs affectionately.)* Still up to your old tricks, you old beggar! I can remember how you used to come up here to mope and dream in the old days.

Robert *(with a smile)*. I come up here now because it's the coolest place on the farm. I've given up dreaming.

Andrew *(grinning)*. I don't believe it. You can't have changed that much. *(After a pause—with boyish enthusiasm)* Say, it sure brings back old times to be up here with you having a chin all by our lonesome again. I feel great being back home.

Robert. It's great for us to have you back.

Andrew *(after a pause—meaningly)*. I've been looking over the old place with Ruth. Things don't seem to be—.

Robert *(his face flushing—interrupts his brother shortly)*. Never mind the farm! Let's talk about something interesting. This is the first chance I've had to have a word with you alone. Tell me about your trip.

Andrew. Why, I thought I told you everything in my letters.

Robert *(smiling)*. Your letters were—sketchy, to say the least.

Andrew. Oh, I know I'm no author. You needn't be afraid of hurting my feelings. I'd rather go through a typhoon again than write a letter.

Robert *(with eager interest)*. Then you were through a typhoon?

Andrew. Yes—in the China sea. Had to run before it under bare poles[1] for two days. I thought we were bound down for Davy Jones, sure. Never dreamed waves could get so big or the wind blow so hard. If it hadn't been for Uncle Dick being such a good skipper we'd have gone to the sharks, all of us. As it was we came out minus a main topmast and had to beat back to Hong Kong for repairs. But I must have written you all this.

Robert. You never mentioned it.

Andrew. Well, there was so much dirty work getting things shipshape again I must have forgotten about it.

---

1. **under bare poles:** with the sails down.

continued ☞

Robert (*looking at Andrew—marveling*). Forget a typhoon? (*With a trace of scorn*) You're a strange combination, Andy. And is what you've told me all you remember about it?

Andrew. Oh, I could give you your bellyfull of details if I wanted to turn loose on you. It was all-wool-and-a-yard-wide-Hell, I'll tell you. You ought to have been there. I remember thinking about you at the worst of it, and saying to myself: "This'd cure Rob of them ideas of his about the beautiful sea, if he could see it." And it would have too, you bet! (*He nods emphatically.*)

Robert. (*dryly*). The sea doesn't seem to have impressed you very favorably.

Andrew. I should say it didn't! I'll never set foot on a ship again if I can help it— except to carry me some place I can't get to by train.

Robert. But you studied to become an officer!

Andrew. Had to do something or I'd gone mad. The days were like years. (*He laughs.*) And as for the East you used to rave about—well, you ought to see it, and *smell* it! One walk down one of their filthy narrow streets with the tropic sun beating on it would sicken you for life with the "wonder and mystery" you used to dream of.

Robert (*shrinking from his brother with a glance of aversion*). So all you found in the East was a stench?

Andrew. A stench! Ten thousand of them!

Robert. But you did like some of the places, judging from your letters—Sydney, Buenos Aires———

Andrew. Yes, Sydney's a good town. (*Enthusiastically*) But Buenos Aires—there's the place for you. Argentine's a country where a fellow has a chance to make good. You're right I like it. And I'll tell you, Rob, that's right where I'm going just as soon as I've seen you folks for a while and can get a ship. I can get a berth as second officer, and I'll jump the ship when I get there. I'll need every cent of wages Uncle's paid me to get a start at something in B. A.

Robert (*staring at his brother—slowly*). So you're not going to stay on the farm?

Andrew. Why sure not! Did you think I was? There wouldn't be any sense. One of us is enough to run this little place.

Robert. I suppose it does seem small to you now.

Andrew (*not noticing the sarcasm in* Robert's *tone*), You've no idea, Rob, what a splendid place Argentine is. I had a letter from a marine insurance chap that I'd made friends with in Hong Kong to his brother, who's in the grain business in Buenos Aires. He took quite a fancy to me, and what's more important, he offered me a job if I'd come back there. I'd have taken it on the spot, only I couldn't leave Uncle Dick in the lurch, and I'd promised you folks to come home. But I'm going back there, you bet, and then you watch me get on! (*He slaps* Robert *on the back.*) But don't you think it's a big chance, Rob?

Robert. It's fine—for you, Andy.

1. Which statement best describes the situation in this scene?
   a. Robert is sorry that Andrew has returned.
   b. Robert and Andrew have recently quarrelled.
   c. Andrew is sorry that he left home.
   d. Andrew has returned home after a lengthy sea voyage.

   1. _____

continued ☞

2. Which statement best describes the relationship between Robert and Andrew?
  a. They share the same interests and goals.
  b. Robert and Andrew were close when they were younger.
  c. They are bitter rivals.
  d. Robert wants to please and flatter Andrew.   **2.** _____

3. What appears to be the major difference between Robert and Andrew?
  a. Robert's attitude toward faraway places is romantic and poetic; Andrew's attitude is practical and businesslike.
  b. Robert is interested in making money; Andrew is interested in progress.
  c. Robert is calculating and shrewd; Andrew is innocent and generous.
  d. Robert admires Andrew's success; Andrew envies his brother's happiness.   **3.** _____

4. What does Andrew's description of the typhoon contribute to your understanding of his character?
  a. He enjoys the dangers of the sea.
  b. He dislikes hard work.
  c. He is a coward.
  d. He is a realistic person.   **4.** _____

5. What has Robert been expecting Andrew to do?
  a. To become his business partner
  b. To lend him money
  c. To leave immediately for Australia
  d. To stay home and help with the farm   **5.** _____

6. What are Andrew's plans?
  a. To leave shortly for Argentina
  b. To jump ship and go into hiding
  c. To become captain of his own ship
  d. To help out with the farm   **6.** _____

B. Understanding Dramatic Theory. Following is an excerpt by Thornton Wilder, from a preface to three of his published plays. Read it, and then answer the questions that follow. *(10 points each)*

I began writing one-act plays that tried to capture not verisimilitude but reality. In *The Happy Journey to Trenton and Camden* four kitchen chairs represent an automobile and the family travels seventy miles in twenty minutes. Ninety years go by in *The Long Christmas Dinner*. In *Pullman Car Hiawatha* some more plain chairs serve as berths and we hear the very vital statistics of the towns and fields that passengers are traversing; we hear the thoughts; we even hear the planets over their heads. . . .

Our Town is not offered as a picture of life in a New Hampshire village; or as a speculation about the conditions of life after death (that element I merely took from Dante's *Purgatory*). It is an attempt to find a value above all price for the smallest events in our daily life. I have made the claim as preposterous as possible, for I have set the village against the largest dimensions of time and place. The recurrent words in this play (few have noticed it) are "hundreds," "thousands," and "millions." Emily's joys and griefs, her algebra lessons and her birthday presents—what are they when we

continued ☞

consider all the billions of girls who have lived, who are living, and who will live? Each individual's assertion to an absolute reality can only be inner, very inner. And here the method of staging finds its justification—in the first two acts there are at least a few chairs and tables, but when she revisits the earth and the kitchen to which she descended on her twelfth birthday, the very chairs and table are gone. Our claim, our hope, our despair are in the mind—not in things, not in "scenery." Molière said that for the theater all he needed was a platform and a passion or two. The climax of this play needs only five square feet of boarding and the passion to know what life means to us. . . .

—"A Platform and a Passion or Two"

7. In this excerpt, Wilder suggests that he was most concerned about
   a. factual truth   **c.** symbolism
   b. inner reality   **d.** afterlife   7. _____

8. Obviously, Wilder was much dissatisfied with
   a. long plays   **c.** realistic playwriting
   b. conventional stage sets **d.** symbolic playwriting   8. _____

9. According to the passage, *Our Town* was chiefly written to
   a. explain all small towns to the larger world
   b. re-create the essence of ordinary living
   c. explain America to itself, symbolically
   d. create one charming girl for all time   9. _____

10. Wilder indicates that he wants his characters to be
   a. understood by people, without the use of props
   b. plain and insignificant
   c. complex and difficult
   d. serene and peaceful   10. _____

C.   For Composition. In his essay "A Platform and a Passion or Two," Thornton Wilder writes that at first he was merely dissatisfied with the theater of the 1920s. Then, he goes on to say, ". . . my dissatisfaction passed into resentment. I began to feel that not only was the theater inadequate, it was evasive. . . . I found the word for it: it aimed to be *soothing*. The tragic had no heat; the comic had no bite; the social criticism failed to indict us with responsibility." Discuss this statement in relation to Wilder's play *Our Town*. (The first question you might ask yourself to answer is: Is *Our Town* "soothing"? In answering this question, consider *Our Town* in relation to the three elements that Wilder mentions: the tragic strand or theme, the comic moment or theme, and the motif or theme of social criticism versus individual responsibility.)

Analogy Test

MODERN DRAMA

Analogies.   For each question, choose the lettered pair which expresses a relationship that is most similar to that of the capitalized pair.

QUESTION 1. _____
WINNOW : HARVESTING ::
A. trap : skiing
B. lose : surplus
C. sow : planting
D. reap : thresh
E. anticipate : future

QUESTION 2. _____
SALLOW : COMPLEXION ::
A. equitable : agreement
B. solemn : humor
C. happy : jealousy
D. entrusted : thief
E. epicurean : fiasco

QUESTION 3. _____
SARDONIC : CYNICAL ::
A. sapient : droll
B. periodic : ageless
C. wry : serious
D. rough : smooth
E. identical : interchangeable

QUESTION 4. _____
PERFUNCTORY : AUTOMATIC ::
A. sarcastic : ironic
B. cursory : detailed
C. functional : broken
D. handmade : machined
E. prohibited : allowed

QUESTION 5. _____
VINDICTIVE : VENGEFUL ::
A. indicative : indiscriminate
B. flammable : flimsy
C. required : prohibited
D. compassionate : unusual
E. charitable : merciful

QUESTION 6. _____
PLACATE : MEDIATOR ::
A. relate : angler
B. judge : arbitrator
C. question : exterminator
D. fish : anthologist
E. discover : trainer

QUESTION 7. _____
SINEWY : MUSCULAR ::
A. stringy : erudite
B. flabby : bulky
C. weak : solid
D. archaic : obsolete
E. effete : athletic

QUESTION 8. _____
METEOROLOGY : WEATHER ::
A. meteorite : space
B. logic : clarity
C. geology : earth
D. meteor : aurora
E. superiority : inferiority

QUESTION 9. _____
LEGACY : INHERITANCE ::
A. ancestor : forefather
B. legitimacy : innocence
C. progeny : forbearers
D. past : posterity
E. descendants : antecedents

QUESTION 10. _____
ALACRITY : HESITATION ::
A. credibility : honesty
B. criticism : critique
C. break : pause
D. jeopardy : safety
E. lethargy : sluggishness

continued ☞

QUESTION 11. _____
AFFRONT : OFFEND ::
A. bewilder : confess
B. defend : attack
C. criticize : flatter
D. praise : laud
E. approach : retreat

QUESTION 12. _____
SUPPLICATE : DONATE ::
A. regard : ignore
B. kidnap : abduct
C. direct : confuse
D. reveal : appeal
E. oblige : disclaim

QUESTION 13. _____
PRECIPITATION : RAIN ::
A. wine : dregs
B. boredom : vapidity
C. sediment : deposition
D. fog : haze
E. mammal : horse

QUESTION 14. _____
UNOBTRUSIVE : BLATANT ::
A. objectionable : offensive
B. tasteful : gaudy
C. reasonable : modest
D. tawdry : loud
E. tattered : worn

QUESTION 15. _____
UNKEMPT : MESSY ::
A. liberal : stingy
B. flimsy : sturdy
C. shorn : trimmed
D. hardship : luxurious
E. slovenly : groomed

QUESTION 16. _____
BELLIGERENT : OBEDIENT ::
A. irresolute : determined
B. concerned : anxious
C. prudent : compliant
D. barbaric : crude
E. amenable : submissive

QUESTION 17. _____
SILICATE : GLASS ::
A. prehistoric : dinosaur
B. rendezvous : meeting
C. carbon : diamond
D. brick : clay
E. steel : iron

QUESTION 18. _____
PATOMIME : MIME ::
A. retire : musician
B. compose : violin
C. rehearse : memory
D. sicken : athlete
E. routine : gymnast

QUESTION 19. _____
TRANSFIGURE : METAMORPHOSE ::
A. leap : crawl
B. mutate : stabilize
C. break : retain
D. worship : efface
E. meddle : interfere

QUESTION 20. _____
SACRAMENTAL : CONSECRATED ::
A. sacred : profane
B. secular : temporal
C. wicked : sanctified
D. reverent : irreligious
E. mundane : eternal

Composition Test

MODERN DRAMA *(Pages 934–1004)*

A. *Where the Cross Is Made* (page 951) is said to combine elements of realism and expressionism. Defend this statement with specific reference to the play. Include a definition of both terms in your essay.

B. On one level, *Our Town* (page 964) is simple, straightforward, and easy to understand. On another level, it is subtle and complex. Discuss both aspects of the play with specific reference to its themes and stagecraft.

_____

_____

_____

_____

_____

_____

_____

_____

_____

_____

_____

_____

_____

_____

_____

_____

_____

_____

_____

_____

continued ☞

_____

_____

_____

_____

_____

_____

_____

_____

_____

_____

_____

_____

_____

_____

_____

_____

_____

_____

_____

_____

_____